SUFFERING

by
Dorothee Soelle

translated by
Everett R. Kalin

FORTRESS PRESS
Philadelphia

This book is a translation by Everett Kalin of *Leiden*, copyright © 1973 by Kreuz Verlag in Stuttgart, Germany, an Egänzungsband in the series "Themen der Theologie" edited by Hans Jürgen Schultz.

Library of Congress Catalog Card Number 75-13036

ISBN 0-8006-1813-0

First paperback edition 1984

Printed in the United States of America   1-1813

96   95   94   93   7   8   9   10

Dedicated to the memory of
Wolf-Dieter Marsch,
1928–1972

Contents

Introduction:
The Two Questions

Hear me and answer,
    for my cares give me no peace.
I am panic-stricken at the shouts of my enemies,
    at the shrill clamour of the wicked.

My heart is torn with anguish
and the terrors of death come upon me.
Fear and trembling overwhelm me
    and I shudder from head to foot.

                              (Ps. 55: 2–5, NEB)

Personal anguish like the Psalmist's has been experienced
in every age. To this day people continue to ask questions that
can neither be answered nor dismissed. Why must we suffer?
Can pain possibly have any meaning? Should one learn from
suffering, as antiquity and the Judeo-Christian tradition urge?
Is that even possible? Does our culture deny the value of suffering? Is a guarantee against suffering worth acquiring at all
costs? Should one wish for himself and others a life free from

pain? a life that fades away peacefully in a death free from pain? Is it possible to integrate the manifold forms of pain into a lifelong process of learning? And why is it that some suffering strikes us blind and deaf and leaves us mutilated, while other suffering enriches our life?

It is axiomatic for me that the only humanely conceivable goal is the abolition of circumstances under which people are forced to suffer, whether through poverty or tyranny. The " 'categorical imperative to overthrow all those conditions' in which man is an abased, enslaved, abandoned, contemptible being,"[1] is, thanks to Karl Marx, a demand that no longer needs any defense. The dialogue with the traditional Christian theology of suffering that will be carried on here under the title "A Critique of Christian Masochism" is a battle waged after the war is essentially over. But it is a necessary battle, first because of the continuing effects in society of Christian perversions of love. It is also necessary for critical theology's own liberation. For even when this theology no longer articulates its sado-masochism, it frequently remains under its spell. Even silence about suffering can stem from theological sadism's tradition of despising humanity.

The issue we face today, in my view, is not about the necessity and possibility of eliminating misery but about the persons through whom this process is carried out. *Who* is working on the abolition of social conditions which of necessity produce suffering? Surely not those who are free from suffering. Surely not those who are incapable of suffering, who at the same time have lost the ability to perceive the suffering of others. Neither is it those who are so thoroughly destroyed through continual suffering that they can respond only in helpless or aggressive attempts to flee.

Only those who themselves are suffering will work for the

1. Karl Marx, "Contribution to the Critique of Hegel's Philosophy of Right," *Early Writings,* trans. and ed. T. B. Bottomore (London: Watts, 1963), p. 52.

abolition of conditions under which people are exposed to senseless, patently unnecessary suffering, such as hunger, oppression, or torture. Are we going to ally ourselves with them —or are we going to remain on the other side of the barrier? This book is an attempt to work on this question.

I do not perceive the barrier I have mentioned to be a natural, objectively given phenomenon. It is not because I am white, have more than enough to eat, and belong to the middle class in an industrialized country that I am on the side of those who have nothing to endure and who therefore see no reason to struggle. The place in which I live is not a matter of fate, the class into which I was born no unalterable destiny. "The sins which man commits—these are not his great crime. Temptation is powerful and his strength is slight! The great crime of man is that he can turn at every moment, and does not do so."[2] That he can turn means that he is able to suffer with those who are suffering and to participate in their struggle.

I am writing this book in the months during which the war in Vietnam is ending. I am writing out of the bitterness of those who, in the midst of new American bombing and demonstrations against it, ask themselves, "Why isn't our outcry doing any good? What's the use of protesting? Have we been screaming too softly? Why have we found no allies—as the Swedes have in their prime minister, the Australians in their trade unions, the Americans in some churches? Why were we able to reach so few people? Why was I unable to explain my despair over this mass murder to my brothers and sisters or to my typist, who experienced the bombing of Cologne in World War II? Why couldn't we show Christians who go to church every Sunday where it is that the crucifixion is happening today? And why have the workers in this part of Germany, who certainly know what exploitation means, shown the least con-

2. Rabbi Bunam, in Martin Buber, *Tales of the Hasidim,* trans. Olga Marx, Vol. 2: *The Later Masters* (New York: Schocken Books, 1947–48), p. 257.

cern for the fate of the rice farmers, who have had their fill of exploitation? Have we been screaming too softly?"

One of the causes of our powerlessness will be discussed in this book under the designation "apathy." The ideal of a life free from suffering, the illusion of painlessness, destroys people's ability to feel anything. A person who is serious about the question of who effects change cannot leave open as a secondary matter, to be dealt with under more favorable circumstances, the perspective from which the change-agent operates. The question addressed to suffering cannot be addressed only from the modern perspective that asks about its causes and their abolition. Rather it must be approached as well through the traditional question about its meaning and its function.

In his third thesis against Feuerbach Marx stated that the "materialistic doctrine concerning the changing of circumstances and education forgets that circumstances are changed by men and that the educator himself must be educated."[3] He insists that the "coincidence of the changing of circumstances and of human activity or self-changing can only be comprehended and rationally understood as revolutionary practice."[4] I am applying these thoughts to the question of suffering. The more people anticipate the elimination of suffering the less strength they have actually to oppose it. Whoever deals with his personal suffering only in the way our society has taught him—through illusion, minimization, suppression, apathy—will deal with societal suffering in the same way. The modern question about suffering, focusing on society and directed outward (question one), can only be addressed meaningfully in a context in which the traditional

3. Karl Marx, "Theses on Feuerbach," in Karl Marx and Friedrich Engels, *The German Ideology*, Parts 1 and 3, ed. with an introduction by R. Pascal (New York: International Publishers, 1947), pp. 197f.
4. Ibid., p. 198.

4

question, directed inward and focusing on the individual (question two), is not suppressed.

Question one is: "What are the causes of suffering, and how can these conditions be eliminated?" It is related to question two: "What is the meaning of suffering and under what conditions can it make us more human?" Whoever ignores the abolition of certain forms of suffering that still befall the majority of people will participate in the profitable maintainance of the conditions responsible for this suffering. To the sufferers he'll counsel endurance, thus expressing his inner interpretation of suffering in a way that is downright sadistic. On the other hand, whoever denies that suffering has any meaning and treats the individual (with his "private little woes," such as divorce or death by cancer) merely as part of the socio-economic network, will have to become shattered and cynical.

The two different questions pose methodological problems. According to question one, for example, the discussion of the concept of suffering as a universal problem cannot be allowed. It wouldn't make any sense to investigate the various kinds of misery without looking at their concrete social causes. Hasn't one already started in the wrong place, it could be asked, when he tries to investigate from a single perspective (namely, "suffering") crop failure and war, drought and plague, environmental damage and systematic defoliation? For that treats the causes themselves as secondary matters so that attention is directed away from a particular type of suffering (war, for example) and focused on the universal problem—suffering (and that from a narrow perspective that concentrates attention on suffering's effect on the individual, to the exclusion of societal concerns). Thus "suffering" becomes a metaphysical problem only by removing the instances of suffering from their anchoring in history. This line of argument, engendered by question one, is irrefutable, and therefore in each case I attempt to proceed from concrete contemporary examples of suffering and to include various testimonies about suffering.

And yet the argument appears to me to be false when it takes the form of the exclusion of the universal. The outcome of such an exclusion is the denial that anything at all can be learned from past historical experiences. It turns individual, unique situations into mere statistics under the a-historical point of view that suffering can be abolished. It underestimates the various forms the encounter with suffering can take (for instance, to seek meaning in suffering and "to learn from suffering"). Furthermore, it fails to recognize that possible attitudes toward suffering that were tried in the past can be put to use anew as long as one remains aware of their historical context. Why shouldn't we learn from a different attitude toward a different, but analogous example of suffering?

Connected with this is a further methodological objection that concerns the language of the investigation. If suffering is perceptible only in terms of question one, then, to begin with, all nonscientific language is prohibited. Then economic, social-psycholological, and psychological analysis must replace all earlier possible ways of speaking, for example, philosophical, theological, and symbolic discourse. In that case theological language adds nothing to understanding, and the truth of what is said needs to be demonstrated in nontheological terms.

I recognize that this objection has to be taken seriously. It is necessary to articulate the Christian understanding of suffering in a way that can speak to people who aren't committed Christians or don't live in a Christian environment. A book such as this makes sense only when it is able to say to those who are suffering that they are "blessed" and will be comforted. This happiness of theirs is not dependent on whether or not they think of themselves as Christians. If the Sermon on the Mount is relevant, it must be applicable to everyone.

But surely the insight that we need to operate without

Christian presuppositions doesn't make it necessary to give up all theological language. We cannot give up a language that transcends all that exists or is derivable only from what exists. The need is not to give up theological language but rather to embark on the search for new theological language. Limiting our speech to scientific language leads to an ever increasing silence; "whatever cannot be said clearly," to use Wittgenstein's phrase, then remains untreated. In contrast to this perspective, it is my view that theology, formally defined, has the task of enlarging the borders of our language. A theology that could wrest land away from the sea of speechless death would be a theology worthy of that name.

> Tell it all, brother, before we fall,
> Tell it all, brothers and sisters, tell it all.
>
> How much you're holding back on me
> When you say you're giving all.
> And in the dungeons of your mind
> Who've you got chained to the wall?
>
> Did you put your feet on higher ground
> To avoid life's muck and stone?
> Did you ever kick a good man when he was down
> Just to make yourself feel strong?
>
> Tomorrow just might be too late,
> Now is the time
> To get your jumbled mind straight
> And seek a new design.
>
> Did you ever walk for a crippled man
> Pretending you were lame?
> What made you think one feeble hymn to God
> Was gonna make him call your name?
> Tell it all . . . .[5]

5. Record "Tell it all, Brother" (Alex Harvey) by Kenny Rogers and the First Edition (Reprise S6412).

This book has grown out of a dialogue with the Christian tradition. More than that, it is the attempt of a contemporary Christian to reflect on experiences of faith. Several kinds of language will be employed, as they are in all serious contemporary theology. The methodological prohibition against using theological-symbolic language in our day appears to me to be a demand for one-dimensional thinking. I cannot comply with such a demand, since questions such as those about suffering, even about earlier forms of suffering that have been eliminated, cannot be answered today without use of a "foreign" language.

My task as a theologian encompasses three operations: to translate whatever can be translated into modern scientific language; to eliminate anything that contradicts a commitment to love; to name, and stupidly (*blöde*) to repeat, what I can neither translate nor put aside as superfluous. I'm using the word *blöde* ("stupidly") first in its older sense, namely, "feebly," for our feeble eyes are not capable of seeing what we are speaking about. Then too, I'm using the word in its current sense, because the repetition of sentences we neither understand nor think through is a sign of stupidity.

It is with this in mind that I repeat—"feebly and stupidly" —what is written:

Now at last God has his dwelling among men! He will dwell among them and they shall be his people, and God himself will be with them. He will wipe every tear from their eyes; there shall be an end to death, and to mourning and crying and pain; for the old order has passed away (Rev. 21:3–4, NEB).

1

A Critique of
Christian Masochism

And surely, O Lord, from the very chastisements which thou
hast inflicted upon us, we know that for the justest causes thy
wrath is kindled against us; for, seeing thou art a just Judge,
thou afflictest not thy people when not offending. Therefore,
beaten with thy stripes, we acknowledge that we have provoked thy anger against us: and even now we see thy hand
stretched forth for our punishment. The swords which thou
art wont to use in inflicting vengeance are now drawn, and
those with which thou threatenest sinners and wicked men
we see ready to smite.

But though thou mightest take much severer punishment
upon us than before, and thus inflict blows an hundredfold
more numerous, and though disasters only less dreadful than
those with which thou didst formerly chastise the sins of thy
people of Israel, should overtake us, we confess that we are
worthy of them, and have merited them by our crimes.[1]

1. John Calvin, "Forms of Prayer for the Church," *Tracts and Treatises on the
Doctrine and Worship of the Church*, trans. Henry Beveridge, Vol. 2 (Grand
Rapids: Eerdmans, 1958), pp. 108f.

A MARRIAGE

A woman I know lives in a little Bavarian village with her husband and their three children. Her husband is a weak individual, small in stature and short on intellectual gifts. He has been drinking for many years, and when he comes home he kicks up a fierce storm, taking revenge on his wife for everything life withheld from him. He torments her incessantly. He accuses her of being a whore, yelling by the open window so that the neighbors hear it, waking the children. Often he beats her. She has no life of her own. She is never allowed to undertake anything independently and has no control over time or money. He also tries to take away the support her own family gives her, maligning her before her brothers and sisters. Or, worse yet, when her mother and brothers are visiting he insults them to their faces and throws them out of the house—but this only when he is drunk.

The woman endures this hell. She walks beside a river and wishes she were lying in it. She speaks of suicide, but there's hardly a chance she'll do it. Just thinking of the children is enough to stop her. She cannot be induced to seek a divorce. She suffers.

This marriage belongs to the many that can be dissolved only by death. The woman lives in a Catholic village where divorce is still very rare. It is not only ecclesiastical law that prevents people from getting a divorce, but also an extremely static world view that doesn't provide for such changes, especially when—as in this case—the divorce would have to be initiated by the wife. In addition there is the matter of economic insecurity, or more precisely, the fear of it, for an objective look at the situation convinces one that this extraordinarily capable woman could manage on her own, even with the children. But she lives in an unenlightened society. Her reputation, immensely important in the provincial outlook of a small village, would suffer. If she did get a divorce she would have to move away, losing all her roots. Nor does her family encourage her to get a divorce. People express their rage over the actions of the husband, but the idea that everything that is is the will of God still has deep roots here. And so the woman suffers on, and there is no hope that the situation will change.

We are dealing here with a form of alienation from one's self which can be characterized sociologically as "powerlessness" and "meaninglessness."[2] Powerlessness signifies "the expectancy or probability held by the individual that his own behavior cannot determine the occurrence of the outcomes, or reinforcements, he seeks."[3] The wife in the case we are discussing has given up trying to induce her husband to change his behavior. Too often she has experienced the uselessness of pleas or threats; again and again she has seen that she was unable to influence her husband, despite occasional promises and new starts. The consciousness that one is powerless is a fundamental element in suffering. Every attempt to humanize suffering must begin with this phenomenon of experienced powerlessness and must activate forces that enable a person to overcome the feeling that he is without power. But in the case of this wife, precisely these forces are as good as dead and buried.

Associated with powerlessness is a further dimension of alienation, namely, "meaninglessness." This occurs when "the individual is unclear as to what he ought to believe—when the individual's minimal standards for clarity in decision making are not met."[4] Not to decide, allowing a process to continue once it has begun, means having decided already. But when a person is alienated from himself, clarity for decision making is precisely what is lacking.

2. Melvin Seeman, "On the Meaning of Alienation," *American Sociological Review* 24 (1959), 783ff.
3. Ibid., p. 784.
4. Ibid., p. 786.

The more a person perceives his suffering as a natural part of life, the lower his self-esteem. For example, if people see their jobs as meaningless, if they understand them as an inevitable evil, then this destruction of one connection with life, namely, the one the job provides, makes them unconnected and unrelated in more than just this one area. They are as good as "dead."[5] The meaninglessness they experience affects most other aspects of their lives.

In the language of role theory, "alienation" signifies a social condition which grows out of a "narrowing of role-distance." Some room to move around in, a certain freedom over against the social role "wife," could, in the case we are discussing, only occur under other social conditions, conditions which would allow the wife other role possibilities. To be caught up in one role, without flexibility, predisposes one to suffer. "Alienation from one's self means a narrowing of role-distance and thereby a suppression of necessary personal achievements in playing one's role. This occurs through unduly great pressure to conform to certain behavior norms, a pressure that is expressed in narrow and overly precise role expectations."[6] According to this view role-distance and diversity of roles would be recommended as ways of avoiding social suffering and suffering caused by society. The sufferer is "no longer the master but the slave in his own role-household."

It seems questionable whether role theory is capable of providing sufficient insight into such suffering, suffering that is inflicted by society but perceived as one's personal destiny. What is at stake is not only distancing one's self inwardly from roles, but objectively abolishing them as well. The role of the self-sacrificing wife, the role of the wage earner who has

5. Cf. Eberhard Jüngel, *Tod* (Berlin: Kreuz-Verlag, 1971). The most important thesis of this book is the characterization of death as unrelatedness.
6. Hans Peter Dreitzel, *Die gesellschaftlichen Leiden und das Leiden an der Gesellschaft. Vorstudien zu einer Pathologie des Rollenverhaltens* (Stuttgart: F. Enke, 1968), p. 365.

to "slave away," are not to be mastered by greater distance. The problem of the wife we are speaking about is not the narrowness and over-precision of the role she is expected to perform. The liberalization of sexual possibilities outside of marriage, for example, would not solve her problem as long as she still feels compelled to fulfill a certain role—living in a shattered marriage or working at a meaningless job.

Therefore, in a certain sense, the attempt to analyze the problem of social suffering "in the language of role theory" leads to results similar to those produced by most Christian interpretations of suffering, namely, it leads to a justification of masochism.

DIMENSIONS OF AFFLICTION

The suffering this woman is going through approaches that which Simone Weil calls affliction, distinguishing it from mere pain and from suffering.[7] She analyzes suffering in terms of its three essential dimensions: physical, psychological, and social. "Affliction" involves all three.

Pain that strikes us in only one of these dimensions is not only easier to overcome but, above all, easier to forget. It doesn't leave behind on the soul the traces so characteristic of affliction: the mark of slavery, the "uprooting of life, a more or less attenuated equivalent of death, made irresistibly present to the soul by the attack or immediate apprehension of physical pain."[8] Each of the three dimensions is present in all true suffering. A pain that is only physical leaves no traces behind; if it is removed, for example, the aching tooth pulled, then it is as if the pain was never there. Nor does purely psychological pain reach the dimension of affliction. The mind,

7. Simone Weil, "The Love of God and Affliction," *Waiting For God*, trans. Emma Craufurd with an introduction by Leslie A. Fiedler (New York: G. P. Putnam's Sons, 1951), p. 117. Copyright © 1951 by G. P. Putnam's Sons. Reprinted by permission.
8. Ibid., p. 118.

whose nature it is to flee affliction "as promptly and irresistibly as an animal flies from death,"[9] still has sufficient ways for escape. A suffering that is spared physical pain is still "artificial," "imaginary." Purely psychological suffering "that is not centered around an irreducible core of such a nature is mere romanticism or literature."[10]

True affliction, on the other hand, manifests itself also physically. For example, the woman we're speaking about experiences incessant headaches.

Even in the case of the absence or death of someone we love, the irreducible part of the sorrow is akin to physical pain, a difficulty in breathing, a constriction of the heart, an unsatisfied need, hunger, or the almost biological disorder caused by the brutal liberation of some energy, hitherto directed by an attachment and now left without a guide.[11]

The third essential element in suffering is the social. "There is not really affliction unless there is social degradation or the fear of it in some form or another."[12] The degradation shows itself in the isolation that accompanies affliction. The woman lives in fear of social ostracism, yet *de facto* she is even now not participating fully in the life of the village. She also experiences the social consequence of suffering that Simone Weil observes when she says, "Affliction is ridiculous."[13]

The lack of solidarity with the afflicted is therefore the most natural thing in the world. "If a hen is hurt, the others rush upon it, attacking it with their beaks. This phenomenon is as automatic as gravitation."[14] It is natural for us more or less to

9. Ibid.
10. Ibid.
11. Ibid., pp. 117f.
12. Ibid., p. 119.
13. Ibid., p. 125.
14. Ibid., p. 122.

14

despise the afflicted, "although practically no one is conscious of it."[15]

This observation can also be verified in the case of the woman. The suffering she endures is avoidable; it projects into our world like a fossil out of the past, stemming from unenlightened social conditions. But precisely this idea that things wouldn't have to be as they are, that they could be changed, is a defense mechanism by which we exempt ourselves from confronting present reality. In a certain sense all affliction has an anachronistic character: tuberculosis among the Indians in Argentina as well as the landscape of Vietnam, made to look as barren as the moon. It is not our time, this time of affliction—it can't be true! "Our senses attach all the scorn, all the revulsion, all the hatred that our reason attaches to crime, to affliction."[16] Gratuitous solidarity with the afflicted changes nothing; precise knowledge that such suffering could be avoided becomes our defense against addressing it. Only our own physical experience and our own experience of social helplessness and threat compel us "to recognize the presence of affliction."[17] Our experience of anachronistic suffering, that objectively need no longer exist, alters even our understanding of time. It strips us of all superiority that grows out of a feeling of progress and puts us in the same time-frame with the one who is suffering anachronistically. We can only help sufferers by stepping into their time-frame. Otherwise we would only offer condescending charity that reaches down from on high.

The recognition of the three dimensions of suffering—physical, psychological, and social—is fundamental for probing the problem more deeply. The unity of the three dimensions can be demonstrated by means of many texts and testimonies, best perhaps by means of those psalms that belong to

15. Ibid.
16. Ibid.
17. Ibid., p. 118.

the genre of so-called individual psalms of lament (for example, Pss. 16, 22, 73, 88, 116). The elements of lament keep recurring: illness and physical pain in which people find themselves crushed and dried up; physical and psychological symptoms of dissolution which are often depicted with words like "pour out, empty"; abandonment by friends, neighbors, and intimates; imprisonment in pain so that one no longer has time or place to experience personal or corporate salvation; being in the sphere of death, in its grasp. Suffering, as it appears in the lament, threatens every dimension of life: time to await what is promised, freedom of movement and opportunity for development, vital association with others, food and health and living space as one's share of the land of promise.[18] This kind of suffering has social dimensions—isolation, loneliness, ostracism—as well as physical.

The structure of this context justifies our speaking of "suffering," thus going beyond the scientific diagnosis "pain." The word suffering expresses first the duration and intensity of a pain and then the multi-dimensionality that roots the suffering in the physical and social sphere.

The story of Jesus' passion is in this sense a narrative about suffering. It is falsified whenever it is robbed of one of its dimensions, as has happened in various epochs of church history and art history. It is the story of a man whose goal is shattered. But this despair over his own cause would be incomplete —and below the level of other human suffering—without the physical and social experience the story describes. Without blood, sweat, and tears, without the threat and experience of torture, it would remain on a purely spiritual level. And the disintegration of his company of followers is part of this experience of suffering, for Jesus is denied, betrayed, and abandoned by his friends.

18. Cf. Christoph Barth, *Die Errettung vom Tode in den individuellen Klage- und Dankliedern des Alten Testaments* (Zollikon: Evangelischer Verlag, 1947).

UNCONDITIONAL SUBMISSION

In Christian literature on suffering these three dimensions, especially the social one, are more or less suppressed. Religious pamphlets on suffering proceed from several common fundamental motifs:

Affliction comes from God's hand. The connection between sin and sickness is recognized far too little. Sin is the deepest and most essential root of sickness. The person who is sick fails to recognize this essential cause of sickness and attributes his suffering to "external circumstances, to natural causes." Full health will be realized in the age to come. Sickness is a splendid opportunity to grow and mature inwardly. Don't you feel how God is at work in you precisely while you are sick? The grace that is operative as one suffers is more valuable than physical healing. Affliction is a means of training used by God's salutary love.[19]

It is possible to summarize two tendencies that appear in the material presented in this study. One is the vindication of divine power through human powerlessness. Affliction is regarded as human weakness that serves to demonstrate divine strength. Sickness and suffering are used for a religious purpose. God is "smuggled into [people's lives at] some last secret place."[20]

Corresponding to this tendency is the other, on the human side, to push for a willingness to suffer, which is called for as a universal Christian attitude. A person is denied the most elementary human right, namely, to defend himself and to say, like Goethe's wild rose, "And I won't endure it." Why God sends affliction is no longer asked. It is sufficient to know he

19. These ideas are all quoted from J. Brenning, R. Brocks, Chr. Gremmels, and D. Preiss, "Leid und Krankheit im Spiegel religiöser Traktatliteratur. Eine Problemanzeige," *Theologia Practica* 7 (1972), 302ff., a study that includes a bibliography. Under "Traktatliteratur" they include "'Readings for the Sick,' pocket-size meditation aids, and those brochures, booklets and tracts (distributed in large editions by about 50 publishers) which are offered for sale in special corners of Christian bookstores or distributed free by religious groups in hospitals."
20. Dietrich Bonhoeffer, *Letters and Papers from Prison.* The Enlarged Edition, ed. Eberhard Bethge (London: SCM, 1971), p. 346.

causes it. In this way one represses all other causes of suffering, particularly the social causes, and doesn't deal rationally with the actual causes.

This denial of rationally ascertainable reasons for and causes of suffering is found not only in these theologically shallow and linguistically impoverished devotional booklets. According to the *Theological Dictionary*, as far as suffering is concerned,

It is then man's duty to accept without reserve the anguishing situation, to integrate and transform it into a positive element of his own self-fulfilment (by acting while he suffers and suffering while he acts—the antithesis of passive acquiescence), so that he takes a personal decision for God . . . . In this sense suffering is "willed by God."[21]

It is true that the typical Protestant pattern of impotence-omnipotence receives less accent here because the activity of people as they suffer is stressed so emphatically. It is not God's work with people but the work people are to accomplish in affliction that is denoted with words like "accept, integrate, transform," words that deal with human strength. Nevertheless, in this particular thought-world the idea does not surface that one should battle suffering and eliminate its causes. The father confessor who has learned this (progressive) theology will counsel the woman in our account to take the actions recommended here, to accept, to transform. He will attempt to strengthen her capacity "to suffer to the bitter end and to become personally transformed."

Often, however, this purely individualistic view sidesteps reality because it overlooks other people involved in the situation. However we understand Christ's injunction, "Do not

21. Karl Rahner and Herbert Vorgrimler, "Suffering," *Theological Dictionary*, ed. Cornelius Ernst, O.P., trans. Richard Strachen (New York: Herder and Herder, 1965), pp. 449f.

resist evil" (Matt. 5:39), it is not intended to apply to evil that is destroying others. Jesus criticized with extreme harshness those who make others suffer and lead astray "the little ones"; a millstone is to be hung around their necks (Matt. 18:6). It is really not enough for a person to transform his own suffering "into a positive element of his own self-fulfilment." The marriage we have described is, for one of the partners at least, a veritable hell, and the children who are growing up in that home are systematically learning to despise life. There is no reason to preserve such a marriage, as though God desired this to be done. This is already clear from the fear the children feel, fear they will retain until it turns into its opposite, hatred and contempt for their father. There is no justification for letting innocent people endure such avoidable suffering.

Almost all Christian interpretations, however, ignore the distinction between suffering that we can and cannot end. And, by referring to the universality of sin, they deny the distinction, in a marriage involving guilt, for instance, between the guilty and the innocent party.

To that extent the Christian interpretations of suffering sketched here amount to a recommendation of masochism. Suffering is there to break our pride, demonstrate our powerlessness, exploit our dependency. Affliction has the intention of bringing us back to a God who only becomes great when he makes us small. In that case affliction is seen as unavoidable, as with the wife whose marriage was destroyed, and turned into a fate, thus rendering any change through suffering an impossibility. Suffering is understood to be a test, sent by God, that we are required to pass. It is considered a punishment that follows earlier sins—in an entirely insufficient proportion— —or as a refining from which we come out purified. Theologians have an intolerable passion for explaining and speaking when silence would be appropriate. Arno Schmidt pictures this passion with unmistakable loathing:

And one of the children was almost entirely torn to pieces, neck and shoulders, everything, by two huge shell fragments. The mother kept on holding the child's head and staring in astonishment at the huge carmine pool of blood . . . . The pastor comforted the weeping woman by saying, "The Lord gave; the Lord has taken away." And, damn him, that coward and sychophant added, "Blessed be the name of the Lord!" . . . Have these people never considered that God could be the guilty one?[22]

God is "Leviathan, who wants to enjoy . . . his wickedness." Theologians serve him as "sychophants."

There have been innumerable religious attempts to explain suffering. The difficulty here lies less in the existential interpretation that people give to their pain than in the later theological systematization, which has no use for suffering that hasn't been named and pigeonholed. Thus, for example, in the Old Testament suffering is divided into "suffering that punishes, trains, tests and serves."[23] The fact that in some Old Testament passages it is Yahweh himself who injured, wounded, imperiled, and caused illness is systematized into the proposition that all pain comes from God. In late Judaism an expiatory force is ascribed to suffering, which helps people obtain forgiveness for their sins. A distinction is made between cultic means of atonement, such as sacrifice, attendance at the temple, and blood-offerings, and noncultic means, such as repentance, suffering, and death. Suffering, and here one speaks principally of sickness, poverty, and childlessness, is considered to have greater expiatory force than sacrifice, because suffering affects the person himself in a direct way and not just his property and possessions. Suffering imparts to the pious person the sure hope that his guilt is thereby atoned for and that in the life to come he will receive only reward for

22. Arno Schmidt, *Leviathan* (Hamburg: Rowohlt, 1949), p. 58.
23. J. Scharbert, *Der Schmerz im Alten Testament* (Bonn: Hanstein, 1955).

his good deeds. The ungodly, on the other hand, who are already rewarded here for their few good deeds, have only punishment to await beyond the grave. Thereby the old doctrine of retribution—sin is followed by suffering—has been reversed: atonement results from suffering. To be sure, the structure of a calculable equalization is retained, in fact sharpened.[24]

But these divisions and interpretations, as well as others, fall to pieces in the face of actual experiences. Affliction strikes even the pious. How can it be punishment in that case? The training value of suffering is negligible. The reaction to the real or imagined creator of suffering is pictured in the Old Testament itself as wrath, ill temper. Suffering produces fruits like curses, imprecations, and prayers for vengeance more readily than reform and insight. Suffering causes people to experience helplessness and fear; indeed intense pain cripples all power to resist and frequently leads to despair. It is precisely the Old Testament that corrects again and again theological theories based on the premise that God sends suffering. "For affliction does not come from the dust, nor does trouble sprout from the ground; much more people bring trouble on themselves as the sparks fly upward" (Job 5:6f.).

But such a sensible perception barely disturbs theologians busy trying to interpret suffering. According to Freud, the technique that religion finds helpful in offering a defense against suffering consists in "depressing the value of life and distorting the picture of the real world in a delusional manner —which presupposes an intimidation of the intelligence. . . . If the believer finally sees himself obliged to speak of God's 'inscrutable decrees,' he is admitting that all that is left to him

---

24. Cf. Eduard Lohse. *Martyrer und Gottesknecht. Untersuchungen zur urchristlichen Verkündigung vom Sühnetod Jesu Christi* (Göttingen: Vandenhoeck und Ruprecht, 1955).

as a last possible consolation and source of pleasure in his suffering is an unconditional submission."[25] Submission as a source of pleasure—that is Christian masochism.

THEOLOGICAL SADISM

It is not difficult to criticize Christian masochism, since it has so many features that merit criticism: the low value it places on human strength; its veneration of one who is neither good nor logical but only extremely powerful; its viewing of suffering exclusively from the perspective of endurance; and its consequent lack of sensitivity for the suffering of others. Nevertheless this masochism of the pious is not the worst thing imaginable. For it offered a kind of help for people, as an existential stance, just in those periods in which the possibilities for lessening suffering were not highly developed. Libidinal impulses are, to be sure, perverted by this stance, but they are not destroyed.

The picture changes as soon as theologians, in a kind of overly-rigorous application of the masochistic approach, sketch in as a companion piece a sadistic God. The libidinal and flexible impulses of pious sufferers are now sadistically fixed by the theologians, who make the wrath of God their essential motif. The God who produces suffering and causes affliction becomes the glorious theme of a theology that directs our attention to the God who demands the impossible and tortures people—although this theology can, of course, show no devotion to such a God. There is little doubt that the Reformation strengthened theology's sadistic accents. The existential experience developed in mysticism that God is with those who suffer is replaced by a theological system preoccupied with judgment day. There is no longer any reason "to envy the good fortune the ungodly are enjoying since this will soon be

25. Sigmund Freud, *Civilization and its Discontents*, trans. and ed. James Strachey, College Edition (New York: Norton, 1962), pp. 31f. (Section 2).

brought to a horrible end."[26] The situation is not viewed from the standpoint of the sufferer; rather it is through God's eyes that things are seen and, above all, judged.

Calvin can give this drastic answer to the question why the ungodly have it so good: "Because the Lord is fattening them up like pigs for the slaughter."[27] The resurrection to glory means for the ungodly a resurrection to destruction.[28] This hatred against the ungodly, destined for punishment, is rooted in a deep self-hatred. Calvin's liturgical prayers abound with self-abasement, humiliation, and insults against humanity. We are "miserable sinners, conceived and born in guilt and sin, prone to iniquity, and incapable of any good work, and . . . in our depravity we make no end of transgressing thy commandments."[29] We should ask God not to put to our account our many sins and failures which are so immeasurably unworthy that they have called down upon us his wrath. Even people's most intimate approach to God, prayer, is here limited, disparaged, called into question and declared null and void. We "confess, as is indeed true, that we are unworthy to lift up our eyes unto heaven and appear in thy presence, and that we ought not to presume to hope that thou wilt listen to our prayers if thou takest account of the things which we lay before thee. . . ."[30] A Roman Catholic prayer on this same theme of unworthiness says, "Lord, I am not worthy that you should come under my roof; but only speak the word and my soul will be healed." Even this "but" of consolation, of liberation, is missing in these prayers of Calvin's.

In a similar way Calvin robs intercessory prayer of all real fervor and compassion and channels it into submissiveness:

26. Heinrich Quistorp, *Die letzten Dinge im Zeugnis Calvins. Calvins Eschatologie* (Gütersloh: Bertelsmann, 1941), p. 159 (Corpus Reformatorum 80, 190).
27. Ibid, pp. 159f. (=Corp. Ref. 77, 544): "quia Dominus eos instar pecorum saginat in diem occisionis."
28. Ibid, p. 147 (=Corp. Ref. 70, 138), literally "par leur confusion."
29. Calvin, "Forms of Prayer for the Church," p. 100.
30. Ibid., p. 107.

But though we are unworthy to open our mouths for ourselves and call upon them in adversity, yet as thou hast commanded us to pray one for another, we pour out our prayers for all our brethren, members of the same body, whom thou now chastisest with thy scourge. . . . [Bring] consolation to all, as thou knowest them to require it, and [render] thy chastisements useful for the reformation of their lives. . . .[31]

It is in the context of God's holy majesty, on the one hand, and people's abysmal depravity, on the other, that Calvin locates his understanding of suffering: the "scriptures teach us that Pestilence, War, and other calamities of this kind are chastisements of God, which he inflicts on our sins."[32] All suffering is attributed to God's chastisement; "the nations whom thou now smitest . . . , the individuals who are receiving thy stripes, . . . [and] all who are bound in prison or afflicted with disease or poverty"[33] must have sinned.

The logic of this sadistic understanding of suffering is hard to refute. It consists of three propositions which recur in all sadistic theologies: 1) God is the almighty ruler of the world, and he sends all suffering; 2) God acts justly, not capriciously; and 3) all suffering is punishment for sin.

It follows from the just way in which the Almighty acts that he torments only "with good reason," even when his torments no longer bear any relation to the wrong that was committed (see the quote on page 9). The two presuppositions that God is both almighty and just lead to the conclusion that all suffering has to be punishment for sin. This sadistic perspective is to be distinguished from Christian masochism, for instance as it is found in the devotional pamphlets discussed above, which considers God not only just but loving. Masochism's presuppositions that God is almighty (proposition one), and loving and just (proposition two), lead to the conclusion that

31. Ibid., p. 110.
32. Ibid., p. 106.
33. Ibid., p. 110.

all suffering serves either to punish, test, or train. It is God's way of drawing near to us in order to win souls for himself.

Both sadistic and masochistic theologies of suffering can be criticized because of their first proposition, the omnipotence of a heavenly being who decrees suffering. Perhaps it is possible to conceive of a combination of omnipotence with righteousness, viewed as absolute and perfectionistic, making demands that by definition cannot be fulfilled. There is, on the other hand, no way to combine omnipotence with love. In any case, it is a qualified love, not radical or fundamental, that is thought of in the devotional pamphlets on suffering. The justice of the modern objection against this God is shown by suffering, the suffering of the innocent. And it must be added that in comparison with the enormity of human suffering, all are "innocent." There is misery that totally exceeds every form of guilt; for all guilt put together it would be "too much."

Ulrich Hedinger is right to criticize radically every attempt to think of God as "a God who justifies misery," to reconcile God with misery. Christian theism has worshiped "God the Transcendent One" and "God the Pedagogue"; its "God is separate from misery and he sanctions it."[34] Mystics have tried to get away from the idea of a God separate from suffering, proclaiming a suffering God. That was the most that could be done in the context of a world dominated by deprivation, oppressed through force, handed over almost totally to natural suffering. "But suffering as something against which one can protest, injustice as something against which one can fight, doesn't really appear."[35] Therefore it is not possible simply to reiterate this position.

Of course the criticism of God as the Transcendent One

---

34. Ulrich Hedinger, *Wider die Versöhnung Gottes mit dem Elend. Eine Kritik des christlichen Theismus und Atheismus* (Zürich: Theologischer Verlag, 1972), p. 33.
35. Ibid., p. 49.

and the Pedagogue hits much harder at the position of theological sadism, and not just in the extreme form it takes in Calvin. Its God comes to a sufferer only with pedagogical intent. "The particular stress might vary, sometimes therapy, sometimes correction, sometimes purification and sometimes punishment getting the accent." What this Christian theism has succeeded in producing can be characterized as "insensitivity to human misery" and thereby "contempt for humanity." "There is only sin, only doing what is wrong in the sight of God." Brutality and salvation become brothers, suffering serves to teach obedience, and there is a perfect "alliance between repressive theism and repressive society."[36]

This God is one whose omnipotence and uniqueness are presupposed, whereby he "is relieved of any accountability for affliction and distress; correspondingly, this is put to the account of individual people or mankind as a whole."[37]

Any attempt to look upon suffering as caused directly or indirectly by God stands in danger of regarding him as sadistic. Therefore it also seems to me problematic to ask, "What is the cause of the suffering of the God who suffers with imprisoned, persecuted and murdered Israel," or whether Christ suffered merely because of "human injustice and human wickedness."[38] Jürgen Moltmann has repeated the attempt to show that Jesus suffers "at God's hands," that God causes suffering and crucifies—at least in the case of this one person. On the one hand, Moltmann has carved out the figure of the "crucified God," the "suffering, poor, defenseless Christ," and criticized the ancient ideal of an apathetic God by portraying God as the "God of the poor, the peasants and the slaves," who suffers "in us, where love suffers." But this intention, this passion for suffering, is weakened and softened through the

36. Ibid., p. 54.
37. Ibid., p. 112.
38. Jürgen Moltmann, *The Crucified God*, trans. R. A. Wilson and John Bowden (New York: Harper and Row, 1974), p. 274.

theological system that transmits it. God is not understood only or even primarily as the loving and suffering Christ. He is simultaneously supposed to occupy the position of the ruling, omnipotent Father. Moltmann attempts to develop a "theology of the cross" from the perspective of the one who originates and causes suffering. This correlates with an understanding of suffering as a process within the Trinity, whereby "one of the persons of the Trinity" underwent suffering while another person of the Trinity was the very one who caused it. An example of this kind of theology is instructive: What happened here is what Abraham did not need to do to Isaac (cf. Rom. 8:32): Christ was quite deliberately abandoned by the Father to the fate of death: God subjected him to the power of corruption, whether this be called man or death. To express the idea in its most acute form, one might say in the words of the dogma of the early church: the first person of the Trinity casts out and annihilates the second . . . A theology of the cross cannot be expressed more radically than it is here.[39]

The author is fascinated by his God's brutality. The story of Abraham didn't reach this height of brutality; it was the father of Jesus Christ who first acted intentionally, "deliberately" slaying his son. It is merely consistent mythologizing when "man and death" are thereby gratuitously reduced to a common denominator. God's actions are described with words like "deliver up, toss out, disown and slay."

Such statements, of which one could find dozens of other examples, are still regarded as normal in theology. They need to be compared with Himmler's speech to the SS leaders:

Most of you know what it means to have 100 corpses lying side by side, or 500 or 1000. To have endured this and to have remained decent men in the process—except for exceptions caused

---

39. Wiard Popkes, *Christus Traditus. Eine Untersuchung zum Begriff der Dahingabe im Neuen Testament* (1967), pp. 286f. (cited from Moltmann, ibid., p. 241).

by human weakness—this has made us hard as nails. This is a glorious page in our history that has never been written and never will be. . . .[40]

Not that theological sadism would offer instructions on behavior. But it does school people in thought patterns that regard sadistic behavior as normal, in which one worships, honors, and loves a being whose "radicality," "intentionality," and "greatest sharpness" is that he slays. The ultimate conclusion of theological sadism is worshiping the executioner.

THE SACRIFICE OF ISAAC

One can get a clear picture of what that means by looking at various possible interpretations of the story of Abraham's sacrifice of Isaac (Gen. 22).[41] The first explanation starts with God. God is the Totally Superior One, the Absolute. Without assuming a visible form he appears in the summons to Abraham. Summons and command are his forms of expression. The question doesn't even arise whether it really is God who commands such things rather than the devil. God is the Lord, and is accountable to no one. He has given Abraham his only son and has the right to demand him back. In terms of this explanation it is precisely the absurdity of the demand that points to its divinity.

If one transfers this explanation to the story of Jesus—a transfer that was carried out very early through the allegorical interpretation of the Old Testament, although the Bible itself did not carry it out—the stress is put upon the father who offers up his beloved only son. The necessity that brings him to do this is reflected upon just as little, or just as unsuc-

40. Heinrich Himmler, Address at a meeting of SS Group Leaders in Posen, October 4, 1943, cited from Walther Hofer, *Der Nationalsozialismus. Dokumente 1933–45*, Fischerbuch, 172 (Frankfurt: Fischer Bücherei, 1957).
41. I'm not going into the history of the interpretation of this passage, but I would like to call attention to the literary interpretation by Erich Auerbach, *Mimesis: The Representation of Reality in Western Literature*, trans. Willard R. Trask (Princeton: Princeton University Press, 1953).

cessfully, as is the necessity of that first command to Abraham. But since in this case the sacrifice is bloodily carried out—and not prevented at the last moment by the very God who had commanded it—the delight this God takes in annihilation moves to center stage.

This explanation of the story contains a sadistic understanding of God. A theology of suffering that is developed from this starting point will necessitate worshiping the executioner.

A second possible explanation remains, to be sure, in the same pattern of command and obedience, of master and slave, but its stress is less on God's absurdity than on Abraham's greatness. He appears now as the prototype for all religious existence, the father of faith, the absolutely obedient one. To get a clear picture of what that means, consider a story from the Nazi period, a story about a physicist whose son worked in the resistance and was captured. The Nazis offered to release the son if the father would make a public declaration of loyalty to the regime. The father conducted himself like Abraham.[42]

Søren Kierkegaard discovered in the story of Abraham the "teleological suspension of the ethical."[43] There are situations in which the ethical orientation breaks down, situations in which people carry out a religiously based suspension of the ethical. This produces behavior that, in contrast to the ethical, cannot be made into a universal standard of conduct. Edith Stein went to the gas chamber with other Jews although she had the opportunity to be rescued and although her death benefited no one. The self-immolations of Buddhist monks in Vietnam, as far as we have access to information about them, or that of Jan Palach in Prague in 1968, can be understood in the same way. They carry out Abraham's sacrifice—but with their own bodies. Yet precisely these examples make it

42. I know the story only by hearsay and would be glad to hear from any reader who could verify it.
43. Søren Kierkegaard, *Fear and Trembling*, trans. Walter Lowrie (Princeton: Princeton University Press, 1960).

clear that it is impossible to understand the Abraham story purely from the perspective of absurdity. The situation cannot be explained sufficiently by recourse to the absurd will of God. There are, of course, situations in which the truth of God's will cannot be made understandable or binding. But even in these cases our relationship to God cannot be viewed as an authoritarian bondage. God is not one who desires or commands such sacrifices, even if we admit that in certain situations such sacrifices exhibit clearly the truth of God beyond the sphere of the ethical. This explanation of the story contains a masochistic understanding of humanity, or perhaps more accurately, an understanding of devotion that can go all the way to the sacrifice of one's own life. A theory about suffering derived from this explanation will seek in all suffering conscious and obedient sacrifice.

But there is still a third way to understand the story, and that is from the point of view of the writer. The writer is trying to overcome the archaic picture of God as one who is pleased with human sacrifices. God is not one who commands the absurd, even though that appears to be the case. People are not compelled to suspend the ethical. The story recalls something from the past—in order to abolish it. The relationship between God and people is misconstrued when it is seen as the absurdity of the command or as the submission of total obedience. In this connection the story's opening statement is especially significant: "After these things God tested Abraham" (Gen. 22:1). In this way an understanding is established between the writer and the reader; we know more than Abraham could have known.

In ancient mythology there is a parallel story of a father's sacrifice of his child. Agamemnon sacrifices his daughter Iphigenia in Aulis, to gain the favor of Artemis, so that she will provide wind for the Greek flotilla waiting to sail for Troy. It is a tragic conflict for Agamemnon. He's guilty whatever he does. To remain faithful to his comrades he must slay the child. But by deciding to act for the good of the state instead of the family he gains the implacable hatred of his wife Clytemnestra. Upon his return from Troy he must pay with his life for killing Iphigenia.

Abraham's story is not tragic. "Now I know that you fear God," the angel says to him. It was not a matter of choosing between two conflicting values or, to put it in ancient terms, between two gods, but only between the fear of God and disobedience. The test was whether Abraham feared and loved God above all things. When the test is passed, the issue around which the test revolves—child sacrifice—loses its interest. The story has no connection with Abraham's later life; it has no consequences. In contrast to the sadistic explanation, there is now no longer any need to reflect on the absurdity of the command. But even the masochism of obedience turns into a useful factor that is subordinated to the renewing and strengthening blessing. Animal sacrifice replaces human sacrifice, just as at a later time incense and rams will be replaced by "my prayers and hymns" (Paul Gerhardt). A humorous variant of the way Abraham learns of the change in plans occurs in a tapestry from the year 1710 that hangs in the Jesuit dispensary in Trier. Isaac is bound on the altar, Abraham is kneeling in front of him a few steps away, his flint-lock in his hand, taking aim. But a little angel is peeing in a high arc onto the firing pin:

> Abraham, you aim in vain,
> An angel sends a little rain.

The theological attempt to understand the story with reference to Christ is now to be evaluated from this point of view, that the story's intention is to enlighten. The humane progress that is pictured in the story in Gen. 22 is negated in the "radical theology of the cross," the intention of the story reversed.

In a theology of this kind the story of Abraham serves as a preliminary stage which has not yet reached the "full severity." Only on Golgotha does Moriah find fulfillment; only there does God strike the final blow. The comparatively weak expression of Paul's that God did not spare his own son but offered him up is now taken to its logical conclusion, namely annihilation.

Who wants such a God? Who gains anything from him? What kind of people must those be whose highest being sees his honor in practicing retaliation in a ratio of one to 100? Why, in such a theology, should Jesus suffer "at God's hands"? Did the victims at Auschwitz die at God's hands, and not because of Cyclone Beta, which the IG-Farben Company manufactured for a few cents a dose? Was he on the side of the executioner—or still on the side of the dying? When you look at human suffering concretely you destroy all innocence, all neutrality, every attempt to say, "It wasn't I; there was nothing I could do; I didn't know." In the face of suffering you are either with the victim or the executioner—there is no other option. Therefore that explanation of suffering that looks away from the victim and identifies itself with a righteousness that is supposed to stand behind the suffering has already taken a step in the direction of theological sadism, which wants to understand God as the torturer.

2

A Critique of
Post-Christian Apathy

The real exile of Israel in Egypt was that they had learned to endure it.[1]

"PRISONERS DESERVE AT LEAST AN SPCA"

Dom Helder Camara, archbishop of Olinda and Recife in Northeastern Brazil, read the following pastoral letter from the pulpit of his see on May 11, 1972:

Abductions, arrests and deportations, especially of students and workers, are happening more and more frequently in our city. The first reason for our complaint and our intervention as chief shepherd is this: not even the Law of National Security or the decrees from the time of Institutional Act Number Five are being observed. Only rarely do those responsible for the arrests identify themselves, as the law requires, and in no case is there an arrest warrant that has been properly dated, with a statement of the reasons for the arrest and the signature of the proper authori-

---

1. Rabbi Hanokh, in Martin Buber, *Tales of the Hasidim,* trans. Olga Marx, Vol. 2: *The Later Masters* (New York: Schocken Books, 1947–48), p. 315.

ties. The arrests are made either at home or, in the case of workers, on the job, and those making the arrests leave the impression that they are dealing with dangerous terrorists and agitators. Those making the arrests show their true colors by the way they operate, using unnecessary and extreme force. Where arrests take place in private homes there have been cases of forced entry.

Imagine the panic that seizes the families, who haven't a scrap of information about where their loved one has been taken. What is the reason for this disregard of regulations, regulations the regime itself drew up? Why, for instance, is there no notification of the proper military authorities within the time specified by law? Why don't they at least get in touch with the families or other appropriate individuals to let them know, for instance, that they can send clothing, if the victims were led off with nothing but the clothes on their backs?

As shepherds who accept responsibility to God, to ourselves and to those who trust us, we assert that unbelievable physical and moral torture is usually employed.

Once again we record the reason for the mistrust with which the church is regarded and for the measures taken against her. This derives from the fact that we can no longer agree—in the name of so-called social order—with structures of oppression that bring the children of God into inhumane situations.

How much longer will anti-communism have to serve as a pretext for the support of injustices that cry to heaven? How much longer, under the pretext of fighting terrorists, will there be a use of terrorism by the police and military authorities?

Leave aside for the moment that this way of operating violates the most elementary human rights. Can we not ask . . . that the victims at least be treated according to the laws preventing cruelty to animals?

We are intentionally writing this letter on the first of May. This is not only because workers comprise the majority of those who are persecuted and that the church in increasing measure has workers in its care. No, we want even more to express our alarm as shepherds by calling attention to the fact that the method of development used in our country is paid for dearly by the little people, the lowly and the voiceless. As soon as they raise a legitimate protest they are treated like communists and subversives, and this again degenerates into propaganda against subversion and communism.[2]

The political situation in which this message is meant to have an effect is characterized first by the increasing deterioration of social conditions for the Brazilian masses. All the economic and structural measures that lead to the "development of the under-developed" are carried on their backs. Those who provide foreign funds and a minute upper class profit from the reforms that are attempted. In the second place, the arbitrary arrests and the persecution of political prisoners are continually increasing. Deterioration of the situation and intensification of the oppression go hand in hand. In the spring of 1972 Helder Camara succeeded in getting the bishops of the southern region to unite in a sharp public indictment against the regime in Brasilia. Their resolution coincided in basic details with the pastoral letter quoted above. That Camara was not named a cardinal in March 1973, as had been universally anticipated, may be understood as a result of his actions.[3] The suffering of the "little people, the lowly and the voiceless" is not explained here masochistically as testing or sadistically as punishment. Nor is it suppressed with patience, the virtue of so many church leaders, or, with the help of the most deadeningly general formulations, turned into a high sounding liturgy. The suffering is expressed. It is indicted. Camara uses words like "complaint, intervention, assert, record, legitimate protest." The situation in which one is content to explain suffering, to interpret it, is overcome. The causes of the suffering are named: the "so-called" social order, the structures of oppression, anti-communism as a pretext for terrorism.

God the Transcendent One and God the Pedagogue, both

2. Quoted from the *Frankfurter Rundschau*, June 13, 1972. The original text, in Portugese, is available in the Bulletin of the Northeast Region II of the National Conference of Brazilian Bishops, #35 (1972), pp. 48f.
3. *Publik-Forum*, March 1973.

of whom justify misery, no longer have any business here. God is on the side of the oppressed, the workers, the "little people."

But who besides him? I'm not speaking about the reaction to the bishops' resolution in Latin America but rather about our response to statements of this kind from the Third World. It is minimal. Indifference to the suffering of others stands in direct relation to the experience that no change is occurring, as people of the "First World" are learning.

This toleration of exploitation, oppression, and injustice points to a condition lying like a pall over the whole of society; it is apathy, an unconcern that is incapable of suffering.

THE APATHY OF SOCIETY

Apatheia is a Greek word that literally means nonsuffering, freedom from suffering, a creature's inability to suffer. According to the lexicon the term relates to certain symptoms of illness and is translated "insensibility, apathy." Medically speaking apathy can "set in as a result of strong psychological or physical exhaustion" (Brockhaus). We are using the term here in a broader sense. Apathy is a form of the inability to suffer. It is understood as a social condition in which people are so dominated by the goal of avoiding suffering that it becomes a goal to avoid human relationships and contacts altogether. In so far as the experiences of suffering, the *pathai* (Greek for the things that happen to a person, misfortunes) of life are repressed, there is a corresponding disappearance of passion for life and of the strength and intensity of its joys. Without question this ideal bears the imprint of middle-class consciousness. But this consciousness extends far into the industrial proletariat. The language of older workers can still label psychical and social suffering clearly. It is more difficult for the younger generation to put suffering into words because apathy has grown with the assimilation of middle-class notions of what to strive for. This doesn't mean that apathetic people in the industrial nations don't suffer—let alone that they are happy. What they lack is an awareness of their own suffering and a sensitivity for the suffering of others. They experience suffering, but they "put up with it," it doesn't move them. They have no language or gestures with which to battle suffering. Nothing is changed; they learn nothing from it.

The plays of Franz Xaver Kroetz deal with conflicts and situations involving suffering among the lower classes, especially the rural proletariat. These conflicts can be ever so extreme, the suffering ever so horrendous—the afflicted face them as though they were miles away, speechless, helpless. There is no understanding of what's going on, no communication, no change. Kroetz' literary technique—long, silent scenes, minimal dialogue, the absence of any word of explanation—makes it clear that there is no hope even for the next generation. These broken people have acquired no insight that they can pass on.

"My characters' most distinctive mode of behavior is silence, for their speech is inoperative. They have no positive intentions. Their problems are of such long standing and are so advanced that they are no longer capable of articulating them."[4] They remain in their state of apathy.

Even expressions of physical pain are repressed. Physical pain is, after all, a sign of vitality and of the refusal simply to accept losses or functional disabilities. To desire freedom from pain means to desire death. In this sense one can understand the apathy of society as part of what Erich Fromm calls its necrophilic orientation. Necrophilia is the love for that which is dead, frozen, motionless, "the wish to transform the organic into the inorganic through 'order'."[5] The inorganic is

4. F. X. Kroetz, *Heimarbeit, Hartnäckig, Männersache. Drei Stücke* (Frankfurt: Suhrkamp, 1971), p. 8.
5. Erich Fromm, *The Heart of Man. Its Genius for Good and Evil* (New York: Harper and Row, 1964), p. 44.

a-pathetic. To change a person into a number in a factory or a governmental bureaucracy is to create an apathetic structure within which every form of suffering is avoided.

One wonders what will become of a society in which certain forms of suffering are avoided gratuitously, in keeping with middle-class ideals. I have in mind a society in which: a marriage that is perceived as unbearable quickly and smoothly ends in divorce; after divorce no scars remain; relationships between generations are dissolved as quickly as possible, without a struggle, without a trace; periods of mourning are "sensibly" short; with haste the handicapped and sick are removed from the house and the dead from the mind. If changing marriage partners happens as readily as trading in an old car on a new one, then the experiences that one had in the unsuccessful relationship remain unproductive. From suffering nothing is learned and nothing is to be learned.

Such blindness is possible in a society in which a banal optimism prevails, in which it is self-evident that suffering doesn't occur. It is part of this self-evident societal apathy that the suffering workers experience is not public, that the problems workers have do not attain the level of public awareness their frequency warrants. Then an inability to perceive suffering develops, not only one's own, through indifference, but especially the suffering of others. The apathy that exists over against the Third World is to be attributed not only to manipulation by the mass media, which can latch on to the prevailing fear of communism and a latent approval of the exploitation of these "lazy" countries. It is also to be seen as part of middle-class apathy in general, which does not even perceive its own pains.

People stand before suffering like those who are color-blind, incapable of perception and without any sensibility. The consequence of this suffering-free state of well-being is that people's lives become frozen solid. Nothing threatens any longer, nothing grows any longer, with the characteristic pains that all growth involves, nothing changes. The painless satisfaction of many needs guarantees the attainment of a quiet stagnation. Boredom spreads if the attainment of that for which one hoped no longer drives one on to a newer, greater hope. Swedish socialism, a pragmatic kind of social system without a utopian vision impelling it on, represents a state of built-in freedom from suffering, which nevertheless produces the highest suicide rate in the world.

In the equilibrium of a suffering-free state the life curve flattens out completely so that even joy and happiness can no longer be experienced intensely. But more important than this consequence of apathy is the desensitization that freedom from suffering involves, the inability to perceive reality. Freedom from suffering is nothing other than a blindness that does not perceive suffering. It is the no longer perceived numbness to suffering. Then the person and his circumstances are accepted as natural, which even on the technological level signifies nothing but blind worship of the status-quo: no disruptions, no involvement, no sweat.

Then walls are erected between the experiencing subject and reality. One learns about the suffering of others only indirectly—one sees starving children on TV—and this kind of relationship to the suffering of others is characteristic of our entire perception. We seldom experience even the suffering and death of friends and relatives physically and directly. We no longer hear the death rattle and the moaning. We no longer touch the warmth and coldness of the sick body. The person who seeks this kind of freedom from suffering quarantines himself in a germ free location where dirt and bacteria cannot touch him, where he is by himself, even if this "by himself" includes a little family. The desire to remain free from suffering, the retreat into apathy, can be a kind of fear of contact. One doesn't want to be touched, infected, defiled, drawn in. One remains aloof to the greatest possible extent, concerns himself with his own affairs, isolates himself to the point of dull-wittedness.

Without question there are tangible sociological causes for growing apathy. There is, first of all, the abolition of shortages of absolutely essential commodities. Hunger and cold as elementary forms of deprivation have disappeared from the industrial nations; needs are satisfied. This private prosperity obscures public poverty and thus helps to cover human suffering. Apathy flourishes in the consciousness of the satiated.

Increasing enlightenment and education are other reasons that some suffering has already been eliminated or become capable of elimination. Greater mobility and increased separation from primary relationships also change the relationship to suffering. We can assume that a divorce will create fewer pains and problems in the future and also that psychological and social pains, like physical ones, will be repressed. This will happen not only through pills and other means of producing numbness and forgetfulness, but also because there is a reduction of the objective causes for psychological anguish. People will be spared social suffering as well as physical. The loss of a marriage partner affects someone differently in a society that constantly holds out new opportunities for making contacts. Greater geographical and social mobility is quite important. Through frequent moves and through career changes people become accustomed to separations. Since fewer and fewer ties are regarded as lasting a lifetime, the dissolution of ties does not evoke the same pain it did in earlier times. Opportunities for contacts have increased, and it has become easier to change the people with whom we have relationships. We are less sensitive to the loss of a friend or marriage partner, and the change brings with it a certain numbness against the pain that such a loss involves. But with this smaller capacity for pain human relationships lose the depth that characterized them in former cultures. A new depth could arise only when secondary and indirect relationships, for instance, to the events in the Third World, would be cultivated and a new sensitivity generated.

THE CHRISTIANS' APATHETIC GOD

The critique of post-Christian apathy would be incomplete if it did not include attention to what prepared its way for so long, namely, the apathy Christians practiced, for which they provided theological justification. The current reproach against Christianity is usually aimed at its masochism, its glorification of suffering that cannot be abolished. But it could be that a much more appropriate reproach today would concern apathy, that "Christianity has become a stranger to pain."

The greatest weakness, irritability, touchiness of a certain kind of contemporary Christianity comes precisely from the fact that whoever has no power over pain is powerless. And anyone who has no acquaintance with pain has forgone the strongest weapon that people in this world possess. . . . Our time is a time of new pains, varied, hidden, unknown pains. They blossom, immense, in the fields of newly discovered reality. Yet we don't see them, don't dare to see them; we crowd them out of our consciousness.[6]

This repression of pains has a long tradition, beginning with the early Christian dispute over the question, "Can God suffer?"[7] The picture of the suffering Christ transmitted by the evangelists contradicted radically the concept of God that came down from antiquity. God was thought of as spiritual, not fleshly; as invisible, not visible; as without origin, not born; as immortal, not mortal; as infinite, not finite; and above all, as without suffering, not as suffering.

This apathy of God has its roots in the thinking of antiquity.

6. F. Heer in *Hochland* 50, Part 6 (1958), p. 531.
7. Hans Küng, "Exkurs 2: Kann Gott Leiden?" *Menschenwerdung Gottes* (Freiburg: Herder, 1970), pp. 622–37.

Suffering, *pathai,* belongs in the realm of the earthly, in a narrower sense as suffering and pain, in a wider sense as the emotions, drives, and passions. God is untouched by all these. Neither the drives nor compulsions that follow from them can affect him. He fulfills the ideal of one who is physically beyond the reach of external influences and psychologically anaesthetized—like things that are dead. Understood ethically, his apathy signifies his spirit's freedom from internal needs and external injuries. According to Aristotle one aspect of God's perfection is that he has no need for friends.[8] This apathetic God became the God of the Christians, although he was a contradiction to the biblical God, with his emotions and suffering. The axiom that God was incapable of suffering became more and more acceptable. The gospels offered the strongest opposition to this process of accommodation. According to their testimony Christ suffered hunger and thirst, exhaustion and beatings, pain, being forsaken by God and death, and he felt love and wrath. In the patristic period, by contrast, there was an attempt to carry through Christ's impassibility as thoroughly as possible (Clement of Alexandria, for instance, denied that Christ really digested and eliminated food!). One attempted to assume apathy and to discover immovability at least in Christ's *soul,* just as one failed to take seriously his fear and his self-acknowledged ignorance. "One inclined towards apathy in Christ's humanity, hoping thereby to protect the apathy of the divine Logos; for a God who would undergo suffering could not be true God."[9] Very diverse conclusions were drawn on the basis of these difficulties. "Some took the suffering seriously at the expense of the divinity, others the divinity at the expense of the suffering. For heterodoxy . . . on the left side it was obvious that Christ endured and suffered . . . but for this very reason he could not be true

8. Cf. Jürgen Moltmann, *The Crucified God,* trans R. A. Wilson and John Bowden (New York: Harper and Row, 1974), p. 268.
9. Cf. Küng, op cit., p. 626.

God like the Father! (Ebionism, adoptionism, Arianism). Fear of violating the principle of apathy was stronger than fear of mutilating the image of Christ in the gospels."[10]

The theological question of whether God could suffer has not been settled to this day. Usually it is resolved in such a way that "one of the persons of the Trinity" suffered, the other two, however, only in him. But more important than such formal dogmatic solutions are the tendencies for an understanding of suffering that come to light thereby. When God is thought of as the Mighty One, as Lord, as King and Judge, then the thought of Christ's suffering emerges only in the sense of the ancient teaching that suffering is a passing evil that serves a greater good. In this thought pattern Christ assumed the form of suffering humanity only for a short time. There is no treatment of the "pain of God" in such a theology. Here the apathetic God has won out over the suffering God, as he did in the Christology of the ancient church. Ethically that means that the stoic concept of suffering triumphs over a Christan concept. When a being who is free from suffering is worshiped as God, then it is possible to train oneself in patience, endurance, imperturbability, and aloofness from suffering. The more a person draws himself back, the smaller he makes himself, the greater are his chances of remaining free from suffering!

The Japanese theologian Kazoh Kitamori has decisively opposed this ruling, apathetic God and attempted to think of God as pain.[11] He sees God as one who suffers because of sin and yet cannot maintain his wrath, who reconciles wrath and love in pain because he loves the object of his wrath, which always entails "suffering." Kitamori criticizes the blindness to pain that prevails in theology and sketches a picture of disci-

---

10. Ibid., p. 628.
11. Kazoh Kitamori, *Theology of the Pain of God* (Richmond, Va.: John Knox Press, 1965).

pleship in which people "serve the pain of God by their own pain."[12] What can such a theological assertion mean? It has meaning only if it includes an interpretation of specific examples of suffering in our society. Where are there people who with their pain "serve" God's pain, that is, his painful love? I hear in these phrases a rejection of all apathy and all patience and submissiveness that grows out of apathy.

People in our society take pain as a fate to which they and others have fallen prey. The significance of every Christian understanding of suffering is precisely the rejection of any notion of a fate into whose grasp people were delivered powerless. "Our pain defeats us, and we fear it . . . because we regard it as an inevitable disaster falling upon us from *outside* us. As long as we try to escape it, we cannot resolve it."[13] This flight from pain into apathy has perhaps in no time been so common as it is now in our highly industrialized society. Suffering is conceptualized as a destiny which one can flee only personally. Fate and apathy belong together in the same way as destiny and the person subject to it. "We can conquer [pain] only when we seek it within ourselves and long for it. We can strengthen ourselves when we earnestly seek and desire pain to be part of our nature."[14] The transformation of pain, in which people move from passivity and flight into acceptance, could signify for the suffering such a "strength," found in pain. But such a theological idea can only become truth when it assumes a political form.[15]

How can we strengthen ourselves? Can one seriously say with Kitamori that we should "earnestly seek and desire pain"? All pain? That would only make sense if it were pain which,

12. Ibid., p. 50.
13. Ibid., p. 80.
14. Ibid., pp. 80f.
15. Cf. Dorothee Soelle, *Political Theology,* trans. with an Introduction by John Shelley (Philadelphia: Fortress Press, 1974), pp. 59ff.

with us as with God, arose out of wrath over historical reality and out of unconditional love for it. Only that pain is good which furthers the process of its abolition. In his interpretation of the parable of the last judgment, in which people are judged on the basis of what they have done to the least of their brothers (Matt. 25:31ff.), Kitamori says:

What we learn from this Scripture passage is that God expects us to love him not as an immediate object, but rather through our neighbors. That is, God becomes *immanent* in historical reality. Moreover the reality denoted here is reality in pain. . . . God becomes *immanent* in these realities of pain: he says, "for I was hungry." Accordingly, service for the pain of God cannot be accomplished by itself, but only through service for the pain of reality.[16]

Our own pain, which we have accepted, will then be related to the pains of the people among whom we live. We stop hoping for a solution from without; that would still be flight from reality and its pains. To "serve the pain of God by your own pain" is to lead suffering out of its private little corner and to achieve human solidarity. Everyone's natural reflex is flight from suffering; but even when it succeeds it is at the same time the perpetuation of universal suffering. To "strengthen oneself" through pain is, on the contrary, to be understood as the strength of those who have achieved solidarity.

I have seen this "strengthening oneself through pain" for the first time in Asia, among people who have become throughout the world the symbol of torment and resistance, the people of Vietnam.

POLITICAL APATHY—IN REGARD TO VIETNAM

The worst form of apathy is not the personal desire to live as free of pain as possible but political apathy. It goes hand in

16. Kitamori, op. cit., pp. 98f.

hand with an astonishing forgetfulness, as though previous generations had not existed and as though their experiences were in vain. The inhabitants of Cologne, for example, have "forgotten" the bombing, at least as far as it related to Hanoi and Haiphong.

Johannes Bobrowski has written a poem entitled "The Elderberry Blossom." With its disks composed of starry blossoms, the elderberry is a symbol of fruitfulness and happiness. The poem deals with the persecution of Jews in czarist Russia and recalls the childhood experiences of Isaac Babel. Only when the poet turns his attention to the young people of a new generation does the motif of the elderberry reemerge:

> People, you say: "Forget—
> Young people are coming,
> Their laughter like elderberry bushes."
> People, the elderberry
> Might die
> Of your forgetfulness.[17]

Apathy doesn't ask about the past because it reacts "naturally." But even nature's smile can fade in an apathetic world.

Apathy over against the history of the Nazi period was only a foretaste of the magnitude of the inability to suffer that has become clear in regard to Vietnam. For my generation, which, politically speaking, spent its youth in the discovery and analysis of the Nazi outrage, the slow realization of what happened in Vietnam came as a shock. To comprehend after Auschwitz that Auschwitz is not over yet, that's what the word "Vietnam" came to mean for us. Even in a direct sense this is the case: genocide, biocide, aerocide, perfected to the highest level of technology, used to annihilate a few million rice farmers;

17. Johannes Bobrowski, "Das Land Sarmatien," *Gedichte* (Stuttgart: dtv., 1966), pp. 75f.

"antipersonnel bombs," which don't damage buildings but are made expressly for people; plastic bombs, whose fragments don't show up on X rays, making it impossible to operate.

But also in another sense Vietnam carries on the story of Auschwitz. For here, as there, people saw, but did not see, heard, but did not hear.

I still remember the day I first learned that American soldiers were present with tape recording equipment as the South Vietnamese tortured "Vietcong" prisoners. They needed the intelligence data in order to carry on the war. It was in the year 1963. Acquaintances I told about it didn't believe me. I looked into the details of the war and soon knew something about the effects of even small amounts of napalm on the skin; about the way one "produced" refugees when they were needed for strategic and psychological purposes; about the privileges an American army unit received whenever it could rack up a high body count (which, of course, included civilian dead). I asked an old friend, who practiced medicine in Hué, how it was determined whether a person was a Vietcong or not. I can still hear his answer: "A dead Vietnamese— that's a Vietcong."

Later, on American television I saw the weekly death tolls, divided into three columns: Americans, South Vietnamese and their allies, and Vietcong. There were no columns for the old, the women and children, who indeed constituted the largest segment of the dead. For every dead soldier this war claimed ten civilians.

There was something else remarkable about this list that I saw at the end of September 1972—the first column was empty. "We've got to change the skin color of the dead," an American general had said. The "Vietnamization" of the war had succeeded; soon thereafter Nixon was reelected and could resume the bombing. In Vietnam I saw him pictured on posters, a frightful green monster, which cast a shadow made up of innumerable skulls. There have not been many days in the last ten years on which I have not thought about Vietnam, about its people and their struggle. The picture of a little South Vietnamese boy behind barbed wire lies under the sheet of glass atop my desk. Napalm, tiger cages, My Lai, "Operation Phoenix," these are words that gradually took the place of Auschwitz and Bergen-Belsen. Often there was the danger that the word would attain a purely symbolic function, "the unavoidable Vietnam," in the language of the right wing. But they didn't know what they were saying. It was indeed unavoidable for us to speak about it. The ultimate political school, that's what it meant for us.

The clearer I became about what was going on, the more I became desperately aware of the apathy on every side. Vietnam was not an urgent topic of conversation. The disclosure of American crimes aroused such a counter reaction ("What about the Vietcong . . . ?"—though there was nothing concrete to point to), that we often chose the less striking examples in the hope, at least in this way, to get people to believe us. Worst of all was the reaction in the churches, where we sought allies. One time as I was collecting money for a hospital in North Vietnam I heard people saying, "For the communists? That's the last straw!" I shot back, "Many are only three years old and have no more legs!" One woman hissed at me, "We give our offerings in the church, not on the streets."

People hardly noticed as they smoothly shifted back and forth between apathy and anti-communism. We often got the impression that only the socialists were capable of suffering. In any case it appears to be one of the practical functions of anti-communist ideology to produce defense mechanisms against contact with suffering. In this way the pain of the exploited in the Third World is minimized, rendered less important, diminished—or else classified in secularized theological categories such as punishment (for laziness and stupidity) or testing (first prove yourselves!).

CHANGE HATE INTO STRENGTH

In November 1972 I accepted an invitation to go to Hanoi. Demolished residential blocks, subterranean hospitals, fields of rubble, bombed-out cathedrals, wretched mud huts on the edge of the city, wounded and maimed people, children (orphaned overnight) wearing the white band of mourning on their foreheads—yet all these forms of suffering were different, for they arose in a different social context and were evaluated by a different standard.

The images of this differing form of life are still vivid within me. I mention only a few of them.

In front of a newsvendor who is almost invisible among the straw hats and bicycles surrounding him, a young boy of perhaps nine squats in the street, slowly and attentively reading the newspaper. His one and a half year old brother, whom he carries around with him in the daytime, as do many older children, waits patiently. Another first impression: a small boy, barefoot, his patched up pants torn again, no buttons on his little shirt, a few school supplies under his arm, the most precious item—a bottle of ink—carefully carried in his hand. These are the riches the poor can afford.

Among the swarm of children who follow us around—curious, beaming, but not obtrusive and self-evidently without begging, there is almost always someone wearing glasses. Though poorly clothed, these children from an undeveloped agrarian country (80 percent of the population are rice farmers) are adequately cared for. They have the advantage of a public health system that discovers and corrects eye defects in children and that, in the few years since its inception (under the conditions of war, blockade, and bombing attacks) has conquered or radically curtailed the most serious "social diseases," as tuberculosis, leprosy, trachoma, and polio are called here.

Poverty is visible everywhere: fabrics are scarce; mud huts on the bank of the Red River remind one of the shanty towns in Brazil: paper, which is in short supply, is gray and of poor quality. Transistor radios are priced out of sight. However, this poverty lacks that characteristic that accompanies being poor in most other countries—it does not humiliate. It does not threaten human dignity, as a favorite Vietnamese expression puts it.

There are two reasons for that. First, elementary needs are met. There is enough rice to go around, together with a high protein fish sauce. There is free health care and preventive medicine.

The other reason that the poverty here doesn't assail human dignity and, comparatively speaking, appears to be quite endurable, is that it affects everybody equally. It is not uncommon to see cabinet members in baggy pants, upper echelon officials in Sunday clothes that may well have been worn fifteen years. Salary differences are strikingly small. We discussed that with the Deputy Minister of Health. He began his answer to our question with a quote: "Ho Chi Minh taught us to treat the patients as if they were our own children. Therefore money doesn't become all-important for us." The starting salary for a nurse is between 40 and 50 dong, of an intern close to 50, of a doctor close to 60. The top salary of an intern is 80 dong, of a nurse 70. A doctor can receive up to 160 dong; a world famous liver specialist, "in a class by himself" as the health minister remarked with some irony, earns 190 dong. Nominally a dong is equivalent to about 30 cents, but actually it is hard to make a comparison since the basic needs, such as rent, light, rice, cost practically nothing. It is public knowledge that Ho Chi Minh received 250 dong, Pham van Dong 240. One can speak of that openly everywhere.

I find it striking that the highly educated minister, who provides information with careful deliberation, starts with a quotation before he gets to the point. We find this to be a common practice wherever we go. Watchwords, sayings of Uncle Ho, moral precepts turn up in everyday contexts as Bible quotes used to among us. "And thus we fulfil the word from the testament of our President Ho." Words are to be fulfilled, legacies appropriated, articles of faith recited. I have never heard the expressions "human dignity" and "encouragement" so frequently as I heard them here. Suffering is constantly present but it has itself become a moral category. "The more they bomb, the better our morale, the more certain our victory." The mayor of Haiphong tells of the 100 children who have become orphaned since the resumption of the strategic bombing of the city in April 1972. Of course we couldn't visit an orphanage, it was said with a trace of irony to counter our assumptions—the children are all living with families. "Ho has taught us to love the children." Their concern with schooling begins with that truth. The weightiest concern after the revolution was how to turn illiterates into readers. The city council resolved to convert into schools all buildings that were still standing and in good condition. To this day the 300,000 school age children are the city fathers' chief concern. Education, morals, instruction, encouragement—the Vietnamese know how to provide a moral framework for living. These are the words of a song about Uncle Ho's voice:

The Vietnamese people take to heart the sayings of Ho Chi Minh. He is an encouragement to us. He spurs us on to overcome all difficulties and to free our beautiful native land.

It is easy to translate that into biblical categories: the people of God, the word, the Spirit who comforts and strengthens, the fulfillment of the word. One is inclined to devalue such a culture as imitative and bound to old images. What can such a model mean any longer in unparalleled situations created by technology? Don't we need innovative educational models, and don't we have to learn to get along without father-figures, even without President Ho exuding goodness and serious-mindedness before a sky blue background? But what one notices here in liberated Vietnam has nothing to do with the justly-criticized brand of traditionalism in the West. For in Vietnam they do not lay down exact and rigid patterns and rules of behavior. Rather Ho (as Jesus) has provided only general guidelines for behavior, while the "fulfillment" of words is left to the creative application each person provides. For this reason there is a different relationship to suffering. Willingness to learn and creativity are sought after.

After a short time all precise codifications are either worthless or harmful. Thus ideas must be formulated again and again, watchwords must be uttered even if they sound as simple as Ho Chi Minh's constantly quoted saying, "Nothing is so precious as freedom and independence."

Such quotable phrases are as necessary as rice. Today Ho is a productive myth, as Jesus the Revolutionary is for priests in the Third World. Perhaps it is the total destruction of confidence in the fathers that leads to cynicism in our world. One component of the feeling of buoyancy and happiness that I experienced in Vietnam was the complete absence of cynicism.

As a European one feels like a barbarian here when one looks at the high regard for art, for the spoken word, for the incorporation of art into life. In a metal factory in Haiphong we heard the workers making music. Someone plays the bamboo flute, another the guitar, the girls sing, at the same time moving to the rhythm of the old and new music. They express their joy, their pain. While the noise of hammers pounding on sheet metal intrudes through the open windows, the twenty year old metal worker Binh Minh ("Dawn") sings, with an incredibly beautiful voice, "Vietnam on the Move." We are speechless. Someone expresses the idea that Binh Minh should receive voice training, but for him singing is not for profit, his voice not for sale. He shakes his head and a colleague quotes Ho Chi Minh's saying, "With our songs we want to drown out the detonation of bombs." The head doctor of a hospital tells us that every hospital has a singing group. "With their songs they bring healing to the patients; it's part of the therapy."

It was also interesting to see the way they handled the rehabilitation of prostitutes who remained after the French left. They were placed in homes where they were systematically pampered, their wishes satisfied, recreation provided. Only after a lengthy period of recovery did propaganda and instruction begin. An analysis of their situation taught them to understand that it was not their fault but that of colonialism that they, as others, were turned into objects for sale. "One has to regain human dignity." Only when that has been successfully accomplished do the women begin to work.

As a result of a universal process of political consciousness-raising, the other women in the society are also able to respect these women. Personal change can have enduring results only in a changed environment. And only where people with such seriousness aim at restoring the dignity of every last lady of pleasure can one speak of socialism. American studies have shown that family structure in South Vietnam is almost totally and, they say, irreparably destroyed. Even the number of prostitutes examined by the state stands at 22 thousand, but that seems to be only a small percent of the total. Whole classes of junior and senior high school girls become prostitutes, the fee set by what grade the girl is in. Will their suffering have any meaning? Will they get a chance to regain human dignity?

In a museum in Hanoi there is a strange casket, resembling a drum, made for a person in a crouching position. On the lid are little finger length metal figures depicting couples making love. It appears to me to be a symbol of the present situation. How tiny and powerless are the people who are transmitting life, how powerful the "President of the United Dead." And yet victory is possible even over this death, which drives surgeons into caves and children into air raid shelters. "On n'arrête pas le soleil" (you can't stop the sun), as Pham van Dong put it later in conversation. "Change hate into strength," stands on a destroyed school. Posters are placed primarily on walls of rubble, on destroyed schools, next to hospitals, and on buildings that have been restored. There are two different styles of posters, 1) emotional-heroic, that at its best reminds one of Fernard Leger, but often reminds one only of very uniform, massive socialist realism, and 2) humorous, with obvious stylistic affinities to the national traditions of Vietnamese folk art. What the "Mice's Wedding Feast" signified for the peasants in earlier times—a feast at which the cats were pacified and slyly satisfied with fish and fowl, singing and stringed instruments—finds frequent repetition today in the portrayals of Nixon, pictured, for instance, as an elephant in the jungle between Laos, Cambodia, and Vietnam. "He's stuck," runs the caption. Or Nixon extending a black, bloody hand: "The USA wants to extend its hand to the nations in friendship." Or Thieu, licking Nixon's boot and saying, "For the past 18 years I have constantly fought for the Republic of South Vietnam's independence." Pictures of this kind, "painted by some of the local residents," are found down to the small villages. According to the words of Ho Chi Minh every inhabitant of the land should be able to paint and draw, to learn a foreign language and make music.

The socialism that is practiced here is vastly different from the East European variety. The experience of equality satisfies an ancient longing. The equality pertains not only to salary but especially to the absence of privileges. A cabinet minister who is flying out of the country waits his turn with everyone else to have his passport and baggage checked; he wears plastic sandals like everybody else. The old revolutionaries in positions of leadership are still clever, unbureaucratic, astute people. Almost all have spent years in the resistance and in French prisons. It is a generation one can spot by looking at faces that mirror privation and clear thinking.

The Vietnamese have a different and uninterrupted relationship to tradition. The constantly repeated history of the people is described in terms of a recurring pattern. Aggressors attack the peaceful people; the resistance grows, led or supported by women or girls; the fight for freedom and independence is a people's war. The fight might be against the enemies from the North, as the Chinese from the feudal period were described; it might be against the Mongols, Japanese, French, or US imperialists. The historical continuity of a brave little people is preserved. A different relationship to suffering can be developed only when the whole people has a vital understanding of its history.

The national consciousness cannot afford to view in negative terms its own history, the values that formerly prevailed, the culture of the people. One does not pursue history here to expose, but to encourage. In the museum we are shown the famous Buddha with a thousand outstretched arms, an eye in each open hand. We are told that this God, the Enlightened One, who sees everything and protects everyone, is very important even for non-Buddhists, for example for Communists who experienced torture. This connection with tradition preserves earlier suffering in the present suffering, earlier struggles in the present struggle. The national heritage is not only dredged up after the revolution as a cultural asset, but the history of the people itself stands under one point of view: protection from oppression, independence from foreign intruders. Suffering has led the people to change. It is understood that through colonialism the entire nation was humiliated and offended. Therefore the class struggle is waged less between the people themselves than in the struggle to resist the colonizers. Pham van Dong told us during a walk through the park at his official residence that during French rule Vietnamese were not allowed to enter this park. A Protestant pastor told me that even the pastoral admonition to avoid alcohol and opium brought a clergyman before the French court.

Another difference from other socialist states is the attempt at decentralization that is made here, in part deliberately, in part by force of circumstances. The sovereignty of the individual provinces is stressed. The communes organize and pay their educational and medical co-workers themselves. The attempt is made to make as many decisions as possible at the lower levels. They improved health care by decentralizing existing medical facilities. The wounded need quick attention, and responsibility at lower levels increases. Even scientific research has been advanced through the circumstances of war. The Vietnamese have an extraordinary capacity for developing what is needed in a given situation: vaccines that keep without refrigeration, and thus are usable even in remote regions; shots for use where there are no bloodbanks; or even the now famous double latrine for the rural population, by means of which parasitic diseases are conquered and fertilizer obtained by natural means. We hear and see little of propaganda but much, by contrast, of instruction, advice, and watchword; much of the attempt, through simple and clear thoughts, to move from theory to practice.

The hours we spend in the beautiful dwelling of the last Vietnamese emperor perhaps bring out most clearly this relationship between the inherited tradition and its actualization in present struggles and suffering. We are guests of the Vietnamese Writers Association. A composer, a sculptress, and some writers welcome us for a cordial and very humorous conversation. "That is Bao Dai's house," someone tells us. "But he doesn't like the house any more, and it doesn't like him any more either." We discuss literature; we read poetry aloud for one another, although we know that to translate is, as a Vietnamese proverb has it, to clip the bird's wings. Te Hanh, translator of the works of Brecht and Heine, reads:

> A stone, not round, not angular,
> A stone like all stones.
> The grave of Brecht.
> The flowers proffer their fragrance
> with respect.
> A stone, simple, pensive,
> Like the poetry you have
> Written in my heart.
> A stone like the countenance of life,
> On which an immortal name has inscribed itself:
> Bertolt Brecht.

We speak about the alienation effect employed by the theater groups who pass through the villages of North Vietnam. A sad pair of lovers looks plaintively at the moon—while a jester keeps running between them, making the audience laugh at his jokes. Someone tells of the lyric poet To Hu, who loves two other poets, Nasim Hikmet and Bertolt Brecht. He says about Hikmet, "His heart burned till the end—his thought emerges from this; in Brecht's case the thoughts burn, and from this a heart emerges." The composer of many resistance songs, Nghuen Xuan Khoat, sings us a song about the old drunk who staggers through the village, keeping time as he sings by tapping with a pencil. He sends greetings to the children in West Germany and encourages them to learn diligently and to write poems. Finally, there is a little speech by the lyric poet Che Lan Vien, an intellectual who knows the Koran by heart and who apologizes that his poems are always almost as long as Hölderlin's. His remarks climax with the thought, "It doesn't do us any good to have beautiful poems if Vietnam doesn't exist any longer. Has our concern been a beautiful culture or independence? What will our descendants say about us?" The petitions and resolutions we had brought with us, which lie on the table amidst tea cups and mandarin oranges, are called by him "great poems"! For him they are part of human dignity. The way he says that when we have independence we have everything brings to my mind the words, "Seek first the kingdom of God, and all this will be added to you" (Matt. 6:33; Luke 12:31). Vien reads from one of his long poems:

> It is not easy
> to be a Vietnamese mother.
> In the world one teaches children
> how to pick flowers,
> and here mothers teach children
> how to enter an air raid shelter.
> In the world one teaches children
> to distinguish the singing of birds
> from noises,
> and here mothers teach
> how to distinguish
> the sounds of jet fighters B7, A7 and F4.
> Dear Mary, for 1969 years
> you have borne your child in your arms.
> Do you know that Vietnamese mothers
> become older and more disconsolate day after day?

Vien turns to me and says, "You will not love the poems that sing about God so much as you love God himself. For the poems have not created God, but God the poems. . . ." Then he tells the story of the 400 transistor radios which the Americans at the end of the Johnson era dropped from the air as gifts for the fishermen. They were accompanied by a letter from the American president, a friendly invitation to capitulate. The fishermen took these radios, with which one could only receive "The Voice of America," smashed them and threw them away. And thus they fulfilled the word of Ho Chi Minh, "Nothing is so precious as freedom and independence."

We are often thanked for the encouragement our visit represents. But in reality it is we who have received encouragement. We have seen a part of socialism about which we always dreamt. We have seen the "capital of human dignity," as Medeleine Riffaud called Hanoi. We have seen affliction, but not in its most terrible form, because the third dimension of affliction, social degradation, was missing here. In its suffering that can hardly be imagined an entire people is drawn together, not isolated and torn apart. Their common history is understood as a process of liberation. Suffering leads not to apathy and submission but rather to productivity. Hatred and pain are transformed.

3

Suffering and Language

Suicide is committed in many cases with incredible orderliness. Preparations for suicide emerge without transition from everyday activities, activities that appear normal, and the suicide itself occurs with the same love for order, same tidiness, the same straightforwardness and mute hopelessness that characterizes the life that caused it.

That speaks volumes about the life of some in our midst, about their unfulfilled expectations, their unfulfillable hopes, their little dreams. That documents their inability to free themselves from their slavery to keep on producing. That shows that their life, their existence is like that of beasts of burden.

Like animals these people communicate their desperate straights by the way they carry themselves. They live in silence, a silence that contains a great deal of order, of patient endurance, of "acquiescing without even being asked," of exploitation and abnegation to the point of impotency and collapse.[1]

1. F. X. Kroetz, *Stallerhof. Geisterbahn. Lieber Fritz. Wunschkonzert. Vier Stucke* (Frankfurt: Suhrkamp, 1972).

FROM THE LIFE OF A WORKER

The following account was written by a 55 year old foundry worker. He describes what he does at the extractor and the general working conditions in a metal factory in Düsseldorf.

That air; it's not exactly pure—that's for sure! Dust, dense smoke, soot; rumor has it that zinc and lead fumes pollute the air and ruin our health. More often than we'd like—especially when the old man melts down a filthy hunk of metal he picked up cheap somewhere—the air is so thick that we have to clear out. The time lost this way has to be made up in a hurry. Doing piece work is really no joke, believe me.

When I get a load of the faces of my co-workers—I used to think it was a laugh—I can also imagine what mine looks like: filth, filth and a layer of filth on top of that. Here and there a little stream of sweat leaves behind a lighter track, which is soon covered with soot again. New drops of sweat roll down, more and more often as the shift progresses. Not only on the face, no, the whole body becomes moist, slippery, green—it's just from copper oxide they tell us. The skin itches from this more than you can bear sometimes. You feel the drops of sweat slide down in spurts on the chest, on the back, along the butt, down the legs all the way to the shoes. Whoever doesn't have sweaty feet gets them at least indirectly this way. Not only the socks but also the underwear, after they've been dried (hopefully) in the locker room, become stiff with salt from the pores, with green-white stripes and spots everywhere. One can't change underwear so often as he'd like; in any case it's all chewed up and disintegrated after two washings. And none of us has the money just to chuck them out the window.

Believe me, folks! You can't always keep the metal from squirting out. Little drops of metal whiz out of the trough like moths around a light. Although I wear gloves my hands always bear the marks of my work: little red pimples, small blisters, third degree burns as big as a penny. One doesn't even bother with things like that any more. Who would run right away to the company nurse, let alone to a doctor, on account of such trifles? You could perhaps lose your job for that.

None of us would like that, believe me!

We're really obliged to wear protective spats to avoid burns on our feet. They are so stiff and annoying, and hardly any air gets through them into the pants. In a word, you'd rather do without them. Only, please believe me, folks, burns on the feet are really somewhat worse than elsewhere. In the metal we work with—mostly brass—there are minute amounts of phosphorus.

I don't know for sure, I could almost damn well believe it, that phosphorus is poison to the skin. The little burns simply won't heal. They keep eating deeper into the skin, in fact they become larger, especially in places like the wrists and knees. After a few days they begin to hurt more and more, until they finally disappear after about six weeks, leaving behind on the skin a blotch that is at first dark but gets lighter and lighter.

When we stand naked in the showers after work I recognize each co-worker by his blotches; no need to look at the faces.

On account of such trifles, on account of oozing, open wounds, do you think we'd take a sick leave? A bandaid does the trick too, believe me, folks! I'm not going to complain, not on account of my crippled hands. You can even get used to that. The doctors for workmen's compensation are really right when they say that in computing our pensions (which we never expect to get). It's only that I have a stupid problem with my legs. The devil knows what that comes from. I hardly think it could have come from work, since I'm only 55. For some years already—the damn thing just won't go away—I've had such a strange feeling in my legs; thrombosis or the like, say the doctors. Are they right? Who knows. I have my doubts about it.

In any case my legs are swollen from something or other, they feel hard; they are red and the skin is slowly peeling away. There are two sores—they're definitely not burns, I'll guarantee that— that are almost as big as half-dollars; they just keep on festering. But I won't give in. Because of them, it's true, I can't always shower after work like the rest. But I take care of them as well as I can. Only I don't go to the doctor any more. The first time he put me on sick leave right away, and I don't want that to happen again. It's possible he might be able to talk me into applying for the disability benefit, and there's nobody to replace me. It would take too long till they could teach somebody new, not to mention the loss in production. No, I couldn't do that to my company. Besides, I need the money, believe me, folks.

But those damn wounds! My legs keep on hurting; sometimes I feel like screaming. Only I'd be ashamed to do that in front of my co-workers. Some of them, it's true, advise me to visit the doctor anyway, before I get blood poisoning, but the others laugh at me, since the pain makes me hop from one leg to the other in my sandals. For it's been a long time since I could wear the safety shoes because of the pain when my feet swell up. Believe me!

If only the air were somewhat cleaner—they promised us an effective exhaust system fifteen years ago. If only the heat were more bearable—they promised to enlarge the building and to leave more room between the machines. But that doesn't happen; just the opposite—they keep cramming in new ones. If only my legs would hold up better, then I could still stand the work.

The heat in the summer is worse than unbearable. Many times you could jump out of your skin, run from the place screaming, become crazy. The air is poison, your throat dry; cigarettes don't taste any good; a hardly describable sweetish taste in your throat downright demands some cool liquid. Experience has taught us that beer is the best remedy for that. Even the boss has no objection to our downing one. His view is that he doesn't know any foundry worker worth his salt who doesn't drink two bottles—during the shift. Through beer, when you get somewhat tipsy, you become oblivious, the job becomes more tolerable. Temporarily the alcohol gets the utmost out of the already overtired body.

Recently I've been preoccupied with gloomy thoughts. My strength is wasting away, and soon I'd like to throw in the towel. When I asked to be transferred to less strenuous work the foreman told me I could sweep the floor if I wanted. I don't want to sink that low again. Besides, that would mean a dollar less an hour, and I do need the money. There's nothing left for me to do but grit my teeth. Indians know no pain.

Believe me! More and more often I get the feeling that they're soon going to throw me away like an old rag. In fact I'm afraid that soon no one will know me, neither the foreman nor my children. Folks, what's left for me to believe in?

I feel an invisible power behind me. Fear? And I'd really still like to click off my ten years and then enjoy my pension.[2]

2. From *Ihr aber tragt das Risiko. Reportagen aus der Arbeitswelt* (Hamburg: Werkkreis, 1970), pp. 35ff.

This is a document about suffering in our time. It is a completely typical case. Neither the specific working conditions nor the psychophysical state of this worker are in any sense unusual or extreme. This becomes clear when you compare it with other descriptions of a worker's lot or look into the statistics on disability.

Physical pain plays a large role in such descriptions. Minor injuries such as abrasions, blisters, burns, take on importance in these accounts because they diminish the person's capacity for work or the amount of piece work he can turn out. What's worse is the exhaustion that grows as the day progresses, exhaustion that arises from the narrowly focused but very intense demand on a few bodily functions. A young Swiss girl writes: "You can feel in your eyes and your arms that quitting time is getting closer and closer. Your eyes ache and you just can't move your arms any longer."[3] Only after years at such forms of work do signs of bodily wear and tear appear. In a great number of cases these aren't treated because the workers are very fearful of being put on sick leave and losing their jobs.

Psychological suffering for the young workers springs first of all from the monotony of the work. Hopes dwindle of being able to learn something on the side or of furthering one's education. There's an ever increasing accommodation to the meaninglessness of the work. Only the younger workers, especially the students in trade schools, still mount any opposition against this kind of work. A seventeen year old female piece worker writes:

Can anyone possibly stand it? . . . Five days a week, day after day, we are swallowed up by the factory for nine hours. . . . I just can't muster the faith to believe that young and older workers enter the factory willingly in order to do the same thing all day.[4]

3. Ibid., p. 108.
4. Ibid., p. 106.

Almost every report shows the workers are oblivious to noise and dirt, foul air and confinement. Because of ever increasing time and motion calculations the job offers fewer and fewer opportunities for varying one's task, and that applies not only to the piece workers. It would be sheer mockery to speak any longer of an "emotional component in playing one's role." The "repressive role-expectations" curb and suppress any remaining possibilities for personal achievement.[5] It is no mere figure of speech to say that workers feel themselves to be part of the machine. That is a precise expression for what happens when personal achievement is not called for. The psychological constriction of older workers ("gloomy thoughts, an invisible power behind me, fear") corresponds to the total hopelessness of the younger workers.

The third mark of affliction as it is depicted here is fear of social degradation ("to sink that low") and of isolation. Among the young workers this fear finds expression in a fear of talking to one another. A part of the burden of suffering is "that folks don't talk to one another." It is an oft observed fact that co-workers laugh at the handicapped or explain nothing to a new worker, that in many cases conversations no longer take place during the breaks and that relationships are not established. The feeling "that they're soon going to throw me away like an old rag" adequately expresses this social dimension of suffering. This worker's account exhibits not only suffering but also dependency. The exploited worker even worries about the loss of production that the employer incurs when a worker who is all used up has to be replaced! He even reckons overtime under a "sense of duty," and behind that, just as behind every sentence in his account, there is certainly the fear of losing his job.

5. Cf. Hans Peter Dreitzel, *Die gesellschaftlichen Leiden und das Leiden an der Gesellschaft. Vorstudien zu einer Pathologie des Rollenverhaltens* (Stuttgart: F. Enke, 1968), p. 326.

And yet his language offers opposition to the external and internal exploitation he experiences. The pathos of the repeated "Believe me, folks!" fights against the reality he is describing. When this plea returns at the end in the question, "Folks, what's left for me to believe in?" this is like a cry for understanding, concern, and solidarity from this worker "swallowed up" by the factory. And though the speaker is scarcely aware of it, therein lies a cry for change as well. All these facts are well known; they have been written about and analyzed. "It often simply cannot be endured," writes a seventeen year old. "And yet I have to endure it anyway. There's nothing one can do to change it."[6] This hopelessness is quite characteristic. The seventeen year old piece worker doesn't consider spending her whole life in the factory. The prospect of getting out through a fortunate marriage, the illusion of soon, next year, no longer having to work, the daydream about her ship coming in one way or another—all of this hinders her more than the young male workers in really coming to terms with her lot.[7] The way a girl is brought up and taught to think ill equips her for spending her life on the assembly line, so she doesn't face what that status involves. It is common knowledge that personal advancement is the only hope capitalism offers workers for abolishing such social suffering. Thereby it demands a corresponding lack of concern for changes that would benefit everyone. The offer held out to a woman is not occupational advancement but love and marriage. Under such social conditions both offers are almost equally illusory. All interests and needs are focused on the individual to an extreme degree, as are all difficulties and suffering. "I" must stick it out, and there's nothing "one" can do to change it; there is no such thing as a "we." It is a social condition in which suffering no longer includes any kind of learning, in which no new

6. *Ihr aber . . .*, p. 106.
7. Cf. M. Herzog, "Akkordarbeiterinnen bei AEG-Telefunken," in *Kursbuch* 21 (September 1970).

change-producing experiences can occur. The expression of many workers that they are "satisfied" agrees with this impossibility of even conceiving of change. It is precisely those who "observe what is going on with sensitivity and precision but have never experienced a change, or else have failed in attempting change, who can no longer conceive of change. The realization that change does not occur is either defended almost aggressively or else one resigns himself to the status-quo."[8]

MUTE SUFFERING

There are forms of suffering that reduce one to a silence in which no discourse is possible any longer, in which a person ceases reacting as a human agent. Extreme external conditions such as exist in camps where people are starving or in destructive psychoses are examples of such senseless suffering. It is senseless because the people affected by it no longer have any possibility of determining a course of action, of learning from their experience, or of taking measures that would change anything. In the German concentration camps the people who existed only in a drowsy stupor, who allowed themselves to be deprived of food, were called in the jargon of the camp "Moslems," doubtless because of their submission to their fate. They are examples of suffering so extreme that it leads to the abandonment of all hope for oneself, to apathy in the clinical sense of the word.

There is pain that renders people blind and deaf. Feeling for others dies; suffering isolates the person and he no longer cares about anyone but himself. Death becomes increasingly attractive in such situations—and one is then no longer capable of wishing for anything except one thing, that everything might come to an end. Just as with bodily pain, a toothache, for instance, all other parts of the body can become unimpor-

8. *Ihr aber* . . . , p. 7 (Foreword).

tant and lose all sensation—the person is all tooth, so this is the case all the more with persistent suffering that presents a threat to life itself, as for instance, in starvation camps. Everything else recedes as unessential, the person becomes totally preoccupied with his suffering, as one does with lust; nothing matters any more outside of the one thing. Extreme suffering turns a person in on himself completely; it destroys his ability to communicate. There is really nothing one can say about this night of pain, whether we find it in insanity or in an incurable disease.

People who vegetate in such conditions cannot be reached by others, though, of course, one cannot stop trying to reach them. It would be sheer cynicism to develop a theology about such suffering, for theology presupposes at least a certain amount of common experience. If it waives that requirement, then it is nothing but talk, and in the worst case its formulations are used to subjugate other people. We can attempt to move this border beyond which language cannot proceed back a few steps, by hearing accounts of extreme suffering with careful attention to their attempts at finding meaning and to their humanity. But we can no more abolish this border than we can abolish the border of death. Respect for those who suffer *in extremis* imposes silence.

Thus theological reflection begins not with extreme suffering but with less radical stages. Unbearable suffering excludes change and learning. Unbearable pain produces only blind and short-lived actions. But when is pain unbearable? When we are struck by disaster our first reaction is that it cannot be endured. Later on we are amazed at how much a person can stand, much more, in any case, than we suspect at the initial moment of horror. This initial phase of pain, which we experience again and again (Phase One), leaves us numb and mute. The weight of unbearable suffering makes us feel totally helpless; we are stripped of the autonomy to think, speak, and act.

We are completely controlled by the situation, and our scarcely formulated lament is more like the cry of an animal.

In our partially enlightened society this suffering that can find no language appears in many forms. It has no way to express itself—aside from numb brooding or sudden explosion. Because institutions and rituals no longer shield the individual by providing him with a language from beyond himself, and because the person fails to carry out a learning process that could rescue him from this stage of muteness, this intense suffering engenders neuroses, frequently also criminality. In such a state a person is incapable of sorting out the individual steps that must be taken if suffering is to be abolished. Thus his behavior remains purely reactive, even his wishes are curtailed. There is suffering which no one can endure indefinitely. Either the person represses it, becomes outwardly indifferent and remains as mute as before, or he becomes sick —or he begins to work on the suffering.

A prerequisite for such work is the conviction that we live in a world that can be changed. Anyone who lives with a static world view, in a post-figurative culture, that is, one that is intent on imitation and repetition of the past (like the culture in which the woman lived whose unhappy marriage we described earlier), cannot see learning and change as the most important things that one can achieve in life. His attitude toward suffering cannot get beyond acceptance and resignation. Only where change itself is comprehended as an essential human value and acknowledged by society, only there can the passive attitude toward suffering change.

PHASES OF SUFFERING

The first step towards overcoming suffering is, then, to find a language that leads out of the uncomprehended suffering that makes one mute, a language of lament, of crying, of pain, a language that at least says what the situation is (Phase Two).

"Believe me, folks!" This worker's description of his lot is an attempt to reestablish communication and to make at least a start towards analyzing the situation. In this he is different from the people in Kroetz's account, who persist in the mute-ness produced in Phase One. He is trying to make his experi-ence fall into place. His capacity for expressing emotions was totally suppressed on the job. Now, as he tells of his pain and his fear, his emotions erupt. The mixture of rationality and emotion is characteristic of such language. A purely rational language, let's say a scientific analysis of the situation, couched perhaps in popular terms, could not accomplish the same thing. It could impart correct information to people, but the stage of mute pain (Phase One) requires more than rational cognition, or rather it cannot make any use of it. First people have to learn to formulate things for themselves.

If one starts with the recognition that the phase of numb pain is the normal one in our society, then it is clear that the phase of expression cannot be skipped as though one could immediately proceed to surmount the suffering through ac-tion. In that way the needs of the sufferers themselves would be skipped as well. Then whatever help they needed—perhaps the achievement of co-determination, even self-determination —would only be imposed on them. They would not have found it themselves and fought for it. They would be helpless in the face of new suffering, arising from some other cause, since their basic alienation itself had not yet been dealt with. This is confirmed by experiences in socialist countries which have not carried on the cultural revolution simultaneously with the revolution in the apparatus of production.

A phrase like "Believe me, folks!" is a modern day psalm. The worker's objectives are not organized as yet; they still appear—as in prayer—as utopian wishes. What is depicted is really suffering, but it is no longer at the stage of submissive-ness. I think of his language as "psalmic language" not so

71

much in respect to a literary genre as to specific elements of language, such as lament, petition, expression of hope. Also characteristic is the emphasis on one's own righteousness, one's own innocence. The repeated phrase, "Believe me, folks!" occupies exactly the same place occupied in the ancient psalms by, "Hear me, O God; hear my supplication." This is the kind of opportunity for expression that the liturgy used to offer in the past.

Liturgy at one time served to give voice to people in their fears and pain, and in their happiness. In this sense one could speak again of worship in the churches if it were possible for a worker, an apprentice, a sick person to express himself there —in the midst of his pain. Then it could be shown that the limitation of the language of the lower classes to the "restringent code" (Bernstein) does not diminish the capacity for expression; quite the contrary. The capacity for expression does not depend on an elaborate code, as can be seen today by anyone who reads the literature produced by workers.

To be sure, the language of Phase Two presses beyond itself, toward change. Therefore it does not merely depict things as they are, but produces new conflicts. An act of self-expression that reestablishes communication between the classes of course intends to be more than just self-expression. The factors that make up the suffering can now be discussed, liberation can be organized (Phase Three). This process itself is painful. At first it intensifies suffering and strips away whatever camouflaged it. It can no longer be toned down, either through displays of humility or through a pessimism about humanity that depicts the suffering as what prevails everywhere, as what is universal. The suffering is now looked at carefully, it is taken seriously, and only under these conditions can the new question arise, How do I organize to conquer suffering? In this phase the expression of suffering solidifies people instead of turning them in upon themselves. Active behavior replaces purely reactive behavior. The conquest of powerlessness—and this may at first consist only in coming to know that the suffering that society produces can be battled—leads to changing even the structures.

PHASE ONE	PHASE TWO	PHASE THREE
mute	lamenting	changing
numb explosive		
speechless	aware, able to speak	organizing
moaning	psalmic language	rational language
animal-like wailing	rationality and emotion communicated together	
isolation	*expression, communication*	*solidarity*
the pressure of suffering turns one in on himself	the pressure of suffering sensitizes	the pressure of suffering produces solidarity
autonomy of thinking, speaking, and acting lost	autonomy of experience (can be integrated)	autonomy of action that produces change
objectives cannot be organized	objectives utopian (in prayer)	objectives can be organized
reactive behavior		active behavior
dominated by the situation	suffering from the situation and analyzing it	helping to shape the situation
submissiveness	suffering	
powerlessness	*acceptance* and *conquest* in existing structures	*acceptance* and *conquest of powerlessness* in changed structures

In this rundown of phases I have refrained from highlighting numb and mute suffering—a common practice that springs from a feeling that silence is a fitting stance for the sufferer before an *almighty* God. A religion deserves to be criticized radically when it claims to give people stability and yet doesn't even teach them to speak, thereby making them neurotic. And of course one is no better off with a positivistic speechlessness, incapable of suffering, that doesn't understand the need to come out of muteness into lament, into expression.

I consider the stage of lament, of articulation, the stage of psalms, to be an indispensible step on the way to the third stage, in which liberation and help for the unfortunate can be organized. The way leads out of isolated suffering through communication (by lament) to the solidarity in which change occurs. The border between communication and solidarity is open, and the steps between the two phases (two and three) can proceed in either direction. The action that produces change keeps experiencing its ultimate limits again and again, but such frustrations need not necessarily lead back to the numb, apathetic suffering that produces muteness. By giving voice to lament one can intercept and work on his suffering within the framework of communication. The hopelessness of certain forms of suffering—whether this is grounded in conditions that are at present petrified or whether it is unalterable —can be endured where the pain can still be articulated. Its language transcends the fulfillment that is within reach in the action of Phase Three, but this transcending is necessary for the sake of what is within reach. Even for the dead there must be cries and prayers.

That sort of thing is conceivable only in the context of a group of people who share their life—including their suffering—with one another. One of them can then become the mouth for the others, he can open his mouth "for the mute" (Prov. 31:8). Liturgies of that kind do not abandon people to apathy.

THE MUTE AND THE SPEAKING GOD

If people are not to remain unchanged in suffering, if they are not to be blind and deaf to the pain of others, if they are to move from purely passive endurance to suffering that can humanize them in a productive way, then one of the things they need is language. Some might say that we are taking a detour if we try to tie our discussion of suffering to the issue of communication, of language. It is true, of course, that one of the fundamental experiences about suffering is precisely the lack of communication, the dissolution of meaningful and productive ties. To stand under the burden of suffering always means to become more and more isolated. Greek tragedy depicts this process by which relationships dissolve one after the other until the individual is finally alone.

However, in tragedy this process does not entail loss of speech. The solitary one turns to the gods or to the powers of nature or he talks with himself. The monologue is not only a dramatically necessary form of speech, but it arises from an understanding of suffering that tradition had developed and that understands the capacity to learn and to change as the decisive reason for suffering.

Thomas Müntzer underscored one of his manifestos with the words:

> Thomas Müntzer will pray to no mute God,
> but only to a God who speaks.[9]

What he means by that is "the living Word of God out of God's mouth" and not only the "Bible apart from experience," which signifies only an "imaginary," a fictitious faith. But the victory over the "mute God" is not confined to the Reformation battle over the scripture principle. The mute God rules

9. Thomas Müntzer, "Das Prager Manifest, November 1521," *Die Fürstenpredigt. Theologisch-politische Schriften* (Stuttgart: Reclam, 1967), p. 15.

today as well, when because of apathy people see no value in putting their pain and their life into words. "That would be boring, uninteresting," was the response of female workers when asked to write about their work.[10] The mute God presupposes people who have been rendered deaf, deaf and dumb.

The sufferer himself must find a way to express and identify his suffering; it is not sufficient to have someone speak on his behalf. If people cannot speak about their affliction they will be destroyed by it, or swallowed up by apathy. It is not important where they find the language or what form it takes. But people's lives actually depend on being able to put their situation into words, or rather, learning to express themselves, which includes the nonverbal possibilities of expression. Without the capacity to communicate with others there can be no change. To become speechless, to be totally without any relationship, that is death.

One of the traditional opportunities a person had for putting his own situation into words, namely, prayer, is today as good as dead and buried. The ability to enter into a dialogue with oneself appears senseless and superfluous to more and more people. This wouldn't be such a problem if a person had new and different possibilities for putting his situation into words, for discussing things, or for choosing to keep silent (which, to be sure, presupposes speech). If, that is, the loss of prayer didn't signify any impoverishment; if monologue, dialogue, and discussion contained everything that formerly was said, stammered, cried, cursed, and wished for in prayer. But is this the case? Isn't the reverse true, that the treasure house of expression and of wishing has been depleted? Hasn't growing apathy increased our muteness? Haven't isolation and fear of one another increased so that communication has diminished, in massive universities and large offices, for example? And hasn't the impersonality of our technological age

10. *Ihr aber . . .* , pp. 102ff.

made it difficult for us to express, or even to recognize, our own desires?

Of course the dialogue a person has with himself still happens. The discourse between the self and the Ideal-self is not to be replaced or abolished. It continues to occur even among those who do not pray in the sense that they turn in petition to a heavenly being. It is not essential to ask what world view a person has, whether he thinks theistically or nontheistically. What is decisive is who the person's dialogue partner is, Christ or mammon or his own vitality. "The result of prayer (the consequent change in the suppliant and his world) depends on whom he is speaking with, that is, in a Christian sense, who his 'God' is."[11] If people experience their life as destined by fate, they are dealing with the mute God, and their prayer can only amount to resigning themselves to their lot. It is above all people's desires that the mute God silences. According to Jean Paul prayer is "desire, only more fervent." It demands that the soul exert itself to the limit; it demands a concentration not only of the will and conscious rationality, but of all our spiritual powers. This virtue, perhaps the most important of all the virtues, and one that can be learned through practice, Simone Weil has called "attention." It "is continually concentrated on the distance there is between what we are and what we love."[12] It is this attention from which creative ability springs, and at its highest level it is equivalent to prayer. "Absolutely unmixed attention is prayer."[13]

As is often the case, religious belief adds nothing here to the completeness and depth of the reality expressed. But it does offer assistance in this discourse that a person carries on with complete attention. For instance, it provides speech forms

11. M. Veit, "Gebet und Engagement," *Ev. Erzieher* 24 (1972), p. 15.
12. Simone Weil, *Gravity and Grace*, with an Introduction by Gustave Thibon, trans. Arthur Wills (New York: G. P. Putnam's Sons, 1952), p. 171. Copyright © 1952 by G. P. Putnam's Sons. Reprinted by permission.
13. Ibid., p. 170.

and traditions about prayer, and it brings to the level of awareness this discourse a person has with himself. But above all, through Christ, the partner in the dialogue, it distinguishes true from false needs and in this way gives to prayer that occurs initially on a natural level a focus that is more comprehensive than personal desires, since it concentrates on "the kingdom of God that is coming."

The loss of prayer, so understood, does not further humanity's liberation, its breaking free of uncomprehended forces. This loss is not a step forward toward an enlightened consciousness, but only a product of that division of labor that turns people into a bundle of functions. The creative capacities and the possibilities for open-ended expression that are potentially there for everyone in prayer are now assigned to a few specialists. Therefore in industrial society prayer is "in itself a subversive act—an act of 'shameless' self-assertion over against this world."[14] It is an act by which people dare to put their desires into words and thereby handle their suffering differently from the way society recommends to them.

Prayer is an all-encompassing act by which people transcend the mute God of an apathetically endured reality and go over to the speaking God of a reality experienced with feeling in pain and happiness. It was this God with whom Christ spoke in Gethsemane.

GETHSEMANE

The name of this olive grove has become a symbol for the suffering that people endure, a symbol for anxiety and agony. "Everyone has his Gethsemane," as the saying goes.

The experience that Jesus had in Gethsemane is reported in diverse ways by the evangelists. Luke attempts to present the experience by including an angel who strengthens Jesus at prayer. But that would make it too easy for us: the miracu-

14. Viet, op. cit., p. 465.

lous always entails the danger of separating Jesus from us, of assigning privileges to him and of ascribing to him a special status he did not possess. Thus Jesus prayed that he would be spared the agony that lay before him. But to this plea he receives no answer. God is silent, as he has been so often in the history of mankind, and Jesus remains alone with his repeated cry, his fear of death, his insane hope, his threatened life.

"My soul is very sorrowful, even to death; remain here, and watch with me" (Matt. 26:38). Even his friends failed to stay with him, friends with whom he shared acceptance and persecution, who shared his conversations and his life. They went to sleep on him like children for whom something dragged on too long. Luke, who is interested in letting them get off somewhat easier, says that they had fallen asleep "out of sorrow." But it is only one more link in Jesus' chain of experience: betrayed, denied, left in the lurch—and, least significant of all, seeing his friends asleep when he needs them.

A person who is afflicted can expect this kind of response from others. During the Nazi period German Jews experienced similar things from their friends and acquaintances. Nadescha Mandelstam portrays the way people acted during the Stalinist purges in the same categories. There were informers who wanted, for instance, to get possession of the victim's apartment; there were good friends who took the phone off the hook when the marked person called; there were co-workers who sent their wives to ask about the person, since they themselves were unfortunately "out of town"; and there were neighbors who slept well when the victim was arrested.

To watch with Jesus, not to fall asleep during the time of his fear of death, which lasts till the end of the world and has in view all the fearful, is an ancient Christian demand that is contrary to every natural response to affliction.

There are two possible misunderstandings of the Gethsemane story, one involving apathy, the other exclusivity.

Attempts to correct the story from the perspective of the apathy-ideal began very early. People tried to make a heroic figure out of Jesus. It was offensive that he cried and trembled, that he endured agony. Already in Luke's account these characteristics of suffering are played down and Jesus' confession of fear to his disciples is omitted. According to Epiphanius, the bishop of Salamis (about 375), later manuscripts deleted the references to Jesus' weeping here and in his announcement that Jerusalem would be destroyed (Luke 22: 43f., 19:41), "out of fear that Jesus' dignity would be diminished." From the modern perspective, however, Jesus' dignity lies precisely in his fear of death. A person without fear is deformed, despising himself too much to be able to have fear for himself. Fear is a sign that a person's roots are planted in life. You have to look out for a person without fear; he is capable of anything.

Apathy is interested in a victorious outcome. But did Jesus go out of Gethsemane as a victor? Did he win the battle? Was he comforted? In the poem "The Garden of Olives," Rainer Maria Rilke defends against that misunderstanding of the story that sees Jesus as a victor who receives heavenly consolation:

> Later it was said: an angel came—.
>
> Why an angel? Alas it was the night
> leafing indifferently among the trees.
> The disciples stirred in their dreams.
> Why an angel? Alas it was the night.
>
> The night that came was no uncommon night;
> hundreds like it go by.
> Then dogs sleep, and then stones lie.
> Alas a sad night, alas any night
> that waits till it be morning once again.[15]

15. Rainer Maria Rilke, "The Garden of Olives," *Translations from the Poetry of Rainer Maria Rilke*, trans. M. D. Herter Norton (New York: W. W. Norton, 1938), pp. 155, 157.

Apathy, at one time the ideal expected of a god, is transferred to nature in this poem. Night, so often a place of protection, of covering, offers no consolation here. It leafs indifferently among the trees, as the manneristic metaphor puts it, meaningless movements of objects that nevertheless remain unmoved. Nature is apathetic, the pain remains for those who are suffering. In Gethsemane Jesus made two futile attempts: he implored his father to spare him, and he asked people to console him. In this night's agony the crucifixion on Golgotha is already experienced. And it is not that watered-down suffering that the church fathers mistakenly pictured as they tried to reinterpret Jesus' cry from the cross, "My God, my God, why have you forsaken me?" (Mark 15:34). Augustine didn't want to take this cry seriously; Jesus couldn't have cried out that way, so it must have been Adam, the first man, crying in him. In Rilke's poem Jesus says: "I find Thee no more. I am alone."[16] Precisely that makes him one with all people and their indifferent neighbors.

The story also has been misunderstood in a second way, from a dogmatic perspective that views the suffering and death of Jesus as unique. One perhaps stresses in such a case that Jesus suffered more than and differently from other martyrs because he saw himself as cast out and cursed, and God was inaccessible to him as he suffered.[17] Jesus' distinctiveness, his incomparability, since they are not to be rescued by reference to an apathy that would make him too lofty to suffer, are here supposed to be kept at least in the *pathein*, the suffering. This way of stating the issue, that in a world of immeasurable suffering wants to isolate Jesus' suffering and make it something that outweighs the rest in order to be able to understand it as unique, is rather macabre. It is not in Jesus' interest to have suffered "the most."

16. Ibid., p. 155.
17. Cf. Jürgen Moltmann, *The Crucified God*, trans. R. A. Wilson and John Bowden (New York: Harper and Row, 1974), pp. 53ff.

On the contrary, the truth of the symbol lies precisely in its repeatability. Jesus' experience, as it stands written here, can befall anyone. Wherever a person is conscious of dying, wherever pain is experienced, there too one's earlier certainty about God is destroyed. People have given testimonies that demonstrate that the symbol can be repeated, that is, that it can be appropriated. They have experienced Gethsemane, the fear of death, but also the conquest of all fears in the place in which the cup of suffering is drunk to the bitter dregs.

One of the most moving testimonies is that of the young Danish sailor Kim Malthe-Bruun who belonged to a resistance group and at the age of 21 was shot to death by the Gestapo on April 6, 1945. During the four months of his imprisonment he turned again and again to the figure of Jesus, trying to grasp what his teaching and his life were all about. In a letter from January 22, 1945, he wrote:

the teaching of Jesus should not be something that we follow just because we have been taught to do so. . . . At this moment there comes to me, as one of the profoundest truths I have learned from Jesus, the perception that one should live solely according to the dictates of one's soul.[18]

The following letter, dated March 3, 1945, reports about torture that he survived, torture that rendered him unconscious. On the next day he wrote:

Since then I have been thinking about the strange thing that actually has happened to me. Immediately afterward I experienced an indescribable feeling of relief, an exultant intoxication of victory, a joy so irrational that I was as though paralyzed. It was as if the soul had liberated itself completely from the body. . . . When the soul returned once more to the body, it was as if the jubilation of

18. *Dying We Live. The Final Messages and Records of the Resistance.* Ed. Helmut Gollwitzer, Käthe Kuhn, and Reinhold Schneider; trans. Reinhard C. Kuhn (New York: Pantheon, 1956), pp. 79f. Copyright © 1956 by Pantheon Books, a Division of Random House, Inc. Reprinted by permission.

the whole world had been gathered together here. But the matter ended as it does in the case of so many other opiates: when the intoxication was over, a reaction set in. I became aware that my hands were trembling. . . . Yet I was calm and spiritually far stronger than ever before.

However, though I am unafraid, though I do not yield ground, my heart beats faster every time someone stops before my door. . . .

Immediately afterward it dawned upon me that I have now a new understanding of the figure of Jesus. The time of waiting, that is the ordeal. I will warrant that the suffering endured in having a few nails driven through one's hands, in being crucified, is something purely mechanical that lifts the soul into an ecstasy comparable with nothing else. But the waiting in the garden— that hour drips red with blood.

One other strange thing. I felt absolutely no hatred. . . .

About three weeks later he wrote:

Since then I have often thought of Jesus. I can well understand the measureless love he felt for all men, and especially for those who took part in driving nails into his hands. From the moment he left Gethsemane, he stood high above all passion. . . .[19]

One of the most precise descriptions of pain in our century comes from the diary of the Italian writer Cesare Pavese, a book that is filled with experiences of suffering. At the height of his success Pavese made the decision to write no more, and shortly thereafter, at the age of 42, he took his own life.

(October 30, 1940)

Suffering is by no means a privilege, a sign of nobility, a reminder of God. Suffering is a fierce, bestial thing, commonplace, uncalled for, natural as air. It is intangible; no one can grasp it or fight against it; it dwells in time—is the same thing as time; if it comes in fits and starts, that is only so as to leave the sufferer

19. Ibid., pp. 80f.

more defenceless during the moments that follow, those long moments when one re-lives the last bout of torture and waits for the next. These starts and tremors are not pain, accurately speaking; they are moments of nervous vitality that make us feel the *duration* of real pain, the tedious, exasperating infinity of the time pain lasts. The sufferer is always in a state of waiting for the next attack, and the next. The moment comes when the screaming crisis seems preferable to that waiting. The moment comes when he screams needlessly, just to break the flow of time, to feel that *something* is happening, that the endless spell of bestial suffering is for an instant broken, even though that makes it worse.

Sometimes there comes the suspicion that death and hell will also consist of pain like this, flowing on with no change, *no moments*, through all time and all eternity, ceaseless as the flow of blood in a body that will never die again.

Oh! The power of indifference! That is what has enabled stones to endure, unchanged, for millions of years.[20]

Pavese presents pain by depicting the time that pain occupies. This time is divided into the waiting and the attack, the waiting for the scream and the crisis of the scream itself. With respect to physical affliction, one alternates between periods with and without pain. Here, too, the observation is quite accurate that one screams needlessly because the "crisis" of "screaming" or the attack, in other words, the high point of pain, is not so bad as the waiting. But Pavese is not attempting to depict pain that is physical in origin, from which one can find respite at least temporarily. Rather he speaks of existential pain which utilizes against us all thinking and feeling, a suffering which brings death.

The Gethsemane story tells of Jesus' pain. Its duration is depicted through the threefold trip back and forth between the sleeping disciples and the place where he prayed. One can think of the repeated praying as the "scream," the absolute

20. Cesare Pavese, *This Business of Living. Diary: 1935–1950,* ed. and trans. A. E. Murch (London: Peter Owen Ltd., 1961), pp. 146f. Copyright © 1961 by Peter Owen Ltd. Reprinted by permission.

high point, and the return to the disciples as the increasingly unbearable waiting for the scream.

Kim also speaks of a double experience he had when he was tortured: the Gethsemane "time of waiting" and the death on the cross, which is easy and transports the soul into a kind of euphoria. It isn't the sacrifice that is difficult. That is something "purely mechanical." So also Pavese says about the attacks that they "are not pain, accurately speaking; they are moments of nervous vitality." What is hard is the "drops of blood" in the period of waiting. We know from reports of people who have survived torture that the torment of waiting for the crisis calls forth all doubts in the person being tortured. The person's own identity is shattered, the pain takes away his consciousness of the cause for which he is suffering, and it leaves the person an empty shell. Why shouldn't one reveal the names of friends? Haven't they long since been arrested? Haven't they themselves long since come clean and confessed? Perhaps in his waiting for the scream Kim experienced the same thing. But for him what is decisive is winning the battle against death. He is now stronger, free of hatred. Love unbounded is nearer than ever before.

It is impossible to distinguish Jesus' suffering from that of other people as though Jesus alone awaited God's help. The scream of suffering contains all the despair of which a person is capable, and in this sense every scream is a scream for God.

All extreme suffering evokes the experience of being forsaken by God. In the depth of suffering people see themselves as abandoned and forsaken by everyone. That which gave life its meaning has become empty and void: it turned out to be an error, an illusion that is shattered, a guilt that cannot be rectified, a void. The paths that lead to this experience of nothingness are diverse, but the experience of annihilation that occurs in unremitting suffering is the same.

Every suffering that is experienced as a threat to one's own life touches our relationship to God, if we use this expression in the strict theological sense. That is, if we don't think of it as an attribute that some people have, like musical ability, but as something everyone possesses, as that "which a person trusts" (Luther). This (nonexplicit) relationship to God is called into question in extreme suffering. The ground on which life was built, the primal trust in the world's reliability —a reliability conveyed in many diverse ways—is destroyed.

The experience that Jesus had in Gethsemane goes beyond this destruction. It is the experience of assent. The cup of suffering becomes the cup of strengthening. Whoever empties that cup has conquered all fear. The one who at the end returns from prayer to the sleeping disciples is a different person from the one who went off to pray. He is clear-eyed and awake; he trembles no longer. "It is enough; the hour has come. Rise, let us be going." An angel came down to Jesus no more than one comes down to other people—or no less than that! Both perspectives are true; Mark and Luke are only using varied ways of putting the matter. One can say that in every prayer an angel waits for us, since every prayer changes the one who prays, strengthens him, in that it pulls him together and brings him to the utmost attention, which in suffering is forced from us and which in loving we ourselves give.

4

The Truth in Acceptance

I heard from old emigrants from Spain about a refugee ship
that was struck by the plague. The captain set the refugees
ashore at an uninhabited spot. Many died of hunger while a
few summoned the strength to walk in the hope of finding a
settlement. One of the Jews had his wife and two small sons
with him. Unaccustomed to such a journey, the wife grew
weak and died. The man carried the children on until he
sank helplessly to the ground. As he awoke he found both
sons dead. In his anguish he arose and said, "Lord of the
worlds! You are going to great lengths to get me to give up
my faith. However, you should know that despite even the
residents of heaven I am a Jew and shall remain a Jew. Even
what you have brought upon me and may still bring upon
me will be of no avail." Then he picked up a little dust and
grass, covered the dead children with it and went on his way
to look for some signs of life.[1]

1. From the Chronicle of Solomon Ibn Verga, "Shevet Yehudah," 1550.

"AND THERE WAS LIGHT"

It is necessary to take a look at the attitude of "acceptance" of suffering that is assumed in the Christian tradition. I mean this not only in a historical sense, in order better to understand the periods in which people saw no other possibilities to diminish suffering, but also in order to learn for our time and to use this tradition to confront our readiness and capacity for acceptance.

The strength of this position is its relationship to reality, even to wretched conditions. Every acceptance of suffering is an acceptance of that which exists. The denial of every form of suffering can result in a flight from reality in which contact with reality becomes ever thinner, ever more fragmentary. It is impossible to remove oneself totally from suffering, unless one removes oneself from life itself, no longer enters into relationships, makes oneself invulnerable. Contrary to what one might wish, pain, losses, amputations are part of even the smoothest life one can imagine—separation from parents, the fading of childhood friendships, the death of certain people who had become especially important in our lives, growing old, the dying of relatives and friends, finally death. The more strongly we affirm reality, the more we are immersed in it, the more deeply we are touched by these processes of dying which surround us and press in upon us.

A significant example of this affirmation is Jacques Lusseyran's life story, which he published under the title, *And There Was Light*. Here on two occasions the utmost threat appears through affliction in its dimensions of physical, psychological, and social destruction. The first threat through affliction occurs when seven-year-old Jacques is blinded in an accident at school. The elemental threat posed thereby for his psychological and social life is warded off by his parents, who treat him like a normal child. He himself accepts the fact that he is blind and lives out his childhood and youth with an overwhelming intensity.

Every day since then I have thanked heaven for making me blind while I was still a child not quite eight years old.

... The habits of a boy of eight are not yet formed, either in body or in mind. His body is infinitely supple, capable of making just the movement the situation calls for and no other; ready to settle with life as it is, ready to say yes to it.

Grown up people forget that children never complain against circumstances, unless of course grown-ups are so foolish as to suggest it to them. For an eight-year old what "is" is always best. He knows nothing of bitterness or anger. He may have a sense of injustice, but only if injustice comes from people. For him events are always signs from God.

... I know that since the day I went blind I have never been unhappy.[2]

However one views this comprehensive, radical affirmation and from whatever physical, psychological, and social causes one derives it, suffering that is accepted and unreservedly affirmed here shows its transforming power. All fatalism about suffering is removed, what is strange, evil, and incomprehensible about the fact that "precisely I" have been struck, becomes unimportant through the power of acceptance. Little Jacques finds "the light" again within himself, he learns "to see," he perceives people with their smells and sounds, and what he calls the "light in me" forsakes him only in situations of uncertainty and fear.

If, instead of letting myself be carried along by confidence and throwing myself into things, I hesitated, calculated, thought about the wall, the half-open door, the key in the lock; if I said to myself that all these things were hostile and about to strike or scratch, then without exception I hit or wounded myself. ... What the loss

---

2. Jacques Lusseyran, *And There Was Light*, trans. Elizabeth R. Cameron (London: Heinemann, 1963), p. 8. Copyright © 1963 by Jacques Lusseyran; English translation copyright © 1963 by Little, Brown, and Company. Reprinted by permission of Little, Brown, and Company in Boston and William Heinemann Ltd. in London.

of my eyes had not accomplished was brought about by fear. It made me blind.[3]

Lusseyran depicts in a parallel case what being blind can mean under other conditions, when acceptance is not achieved.

When I was fifteen I spent long afternoons with a blind boy my own age, one who went blind, I should add, in circumstances very like my own. Today I have few memories as painful. This boy terrified me. He was the living image of everything that might have happened to me if I had not been fortunate, more fortunate than he. For he was really blind. He had seen nothing since his accident. His faculties were normal, he could have seen as well as I. But they had kept him from doing so. To protect him, as they put it, they had cut him off from everything, and made fun of all his attempts to explain what he felt. In grief and revenge, he had thrown himself into brutal solitude. Even his body lay prostrate in the depths of an armchair. To my horror I saw that he did not like me.[4]

The second situation in which Lusseyran experienced extreme suffering involves Buchenwald, the German concentration camp to which Jacques is deported when he, as a nineteen-year-old high school student, is leading a resistance group. He survives hunger, cold, and a period of illness that appears hopeless and then undertakes tasks for the other prisoners, as in the "Defense of France" group. "We had to make war on the disease [of doubt and agony hitting the camp because of false rumors]; . . . how were we to hold on to the remnants of reason in the swirling madness of deportation?"[5]

These are very characteristic sentences. Jacques received information about the military situation for his cell block. He gathered, interpreted, and translated the reports. But more than that:

3. Ibid., p. 12.
4. Ibid., p. 21.
5. Ibid., pp. 229, 231.

I could try to show . . . [my fellow-prisoners] how to go about holding on to life. I could turn towards them the flow of light and joy which had grown so abundant in me. From that time on they stopped stealing my bread or my soup. It never happened again. Often my comrades would wake me up in the night and take me to comfort someone, sometimes a long way off in another block.

Almost everyone forgot I was a student. I became "the blind Frenchman." For many, I was just "the man who didn't die." Hundreds of people confided in me. The men were determined to talk to me. They spoke to me in French, in Russian, in German, in Polish. I did the best I could to understand them all. That is how I lived, how I survived. The rest I cannot describe.[6]

Lusseyran's book is a discussion of how, under extremely favorable psychosocial conditions, suffering can be overcome, whether it is inflicted by natural causes or imposed by force. The distinction between suffering that strikes a person by chance or from natural causes and cannot be alleviated and that entirely different kind of suffering that is created for people by people and that the individual, such as Jacques Lusseyran, could have avoided completely—this distinction plays no role. Lusseyran's power is so unbroken, his acceptance of life as a whole so strong, that he doesn't waste a single thought on avoiding suffering or evading it. The theodicy question is superseded here by an unlimited love for reality.

The primal trust that a child possesses is unbroken, the faith that "all things work together for good to them that love God" (Rom. 8:28) shows itself to be true. The person goes far beyond merely enduring conditions as they are—he lives love for reality, he affirms the totality of his present experience, even its painful segments.

The traditional symbol for this affirmed and loved totality is "God." Lusseyran uses this symbol somewhat self-evidently, without devoting particular attention to it. But this God does

6. Ibid., p. 222.

not operate like the one in the Christian devotional literature, who in suffering "often has to treat us harshly" or "who lets you experience things now for which we might later envy you." Here people are at work accepting reality and transforming it. The question nowhere arises why God caused this or that. This God, the Maker of Everything, plays no role at all. God is the symbol for our unending capacity to love. Here the theme is that about which theology hardly dares to speak any longer, because it has a fixation on that which God gives, brings, promises, or denies us. Here the theme is love *toward God,* toward one who certainly is not over us like a perfect being but one who is in the process of becoming, as is everything we love.

A true acceptance of reality cannot be dragged in surreptitiously by referring to the oft forgotten God who now reports for duty in suffering and death. The prerequisite for acceptance is a deeper love for reality, a love that avoids placing conditions on reality. Only when we stop making conditions that a person has to satisfy before we yield ourselves to him, only then do we love him. It seems to me appropriate that Christian tradition has referred to the love that parents have for their children as an example of unconditional love. One cannot hand pick his children or program in advance what they'll be like or, if they don't satisfy, trade them in. The same thing is true of the relationship to reality, that is, of love for God. It cannot be made dependent on the fulfillment of certain conditions. There is no place here for the *do ut des* principle ("I give in order that you might give"); the "business spirit," as Meister Eckhart calls it, is excluded. As far as love for God is concerned—and nothing else is a total affirmation of reality—perhaps the statement of Philene, the girl of loose morals in Goethe's "Wilhelm Meister," is more readily applicable: "What makes you think that something about you has anything to do with my loving you?"

The affirmation of suffering, when it is not squeezed out of a person, has a mystical core that Philene's statement puts into words in a way that is at once ironic and profound. It is not by chance that mystical elements crop up in all Christian reflection on suffering. One can read Lusseyran's book as a commentary on the great mystical experiences: dying to self, poverty, light within the soul. What disgusts me about the banal theology of the devotional pamphlets is precisely its ignorance about this mystical core. These devotional pamphlets replace mysticism with masochism. They don't demand too much of people but too little, only the acknowledgment of a supreme potentate and not a love that has far surpassed this potentate and his ways, a love that "despite even the residents of heaven" speaks the yes of faith, even against all experience.

MYSTICISM'S THEOLOGY OF SUFFERING

The decisive point in mysticism's treatment of suffering is not, as a superficial critic thinks, its irrationality, which miraculously transforms suffering into a desired good. What is decisive is much more the taking away of power from the one who causes the suffering. The "unveiled face" is a picture Eckhart has for the increasingly indistinguishable "ground" that separates God from man. That love for God can be stronger than every form of affliction, that is the mystical core that in its radical dethronement of the Lord God has to be viewed with suspicion by all priestly theology.

The fear that all "ordinary" theology has of all "mystical" theology has its basis here. Doesn't love that is only human triumph over a more or less impotent God in mysticism? But whoever puts the question this way is himself still caught in the pattern of the powerful and the powerless, who make a deal with one another, a deal that is called "religion." But precisely this deal and this pattern, together with their political consequences, are ended, the "whole business of Other-worldery" is wiped away for the sake of humanity and in humanity.[7] It is no longer the Lord God but another who now serves as "the inmost *state* (not object) of our own misery, our own wandering, our own suppressed glory."[8] Priestly theology answers the problem of suffering with submission. "The Lord has given; the Lord has taken away; blessed be the name of the Lord." Mystical theology answers suffering with a love in view of which the "Lord" has to feel ashamed, for it is stronger than he. But "the Lord" is no longer the object of this theology. Therefore "I pray God to rid me of God."[9]

It is paradoxical but true that unconditional love for reality does not in the least defuse passionate desires to change reality. To love God unconditionally does not mean to deny our concrete desires and accept everything just as it is. To put it in mystical terminology, unconditional love can allow itself the most absurd desires—it can pray for them and it can work for them, precisely because it does not make the existence of God depend on the fulfillment of these desires.

Mystical love, as it appears in Philine's statement or as the old Jew expresses it, transcends every God who is less than love. The concrete expression of such love is not so rare as it might seem. Experience teaches that pain and suffering are in certain situations easily borne or barely perceived. Privations that ordinarily seem unbearable are accepted with ease, dangers unnoticed, fears forgotten. What makes assent to suffering easy and, one could say, self-evident is concentration on a greater cause, whether that is survival or something that is considered to be essential for human life, the freedom of a people, for example. The physical pain of giving birth, which

7. Ernst Bloch, *Atheism in Christianity: The Religion of the Exodus and the Kingdom,* trans. J. T. Swann (New York: Herder and Herder, 1952), p. 64.
8. Ibid., p. 213.
9. *Meister Eckhart*, ed. Franz Pfeiffer, trans., with some omissions and additions, C. de B. Evans (London: Watkins, 1956), p. 220 (Sermon #87).

was used again and again as a metaphor for such suffering, cannot be compared with senseless kidney stones. Mystics have tried to turn all suffering into labor pains and to abolish all senselessness.

It is clear that this mystical core of the acceptance of suffering involves dangers. The ego-strength of loving to an excessive degree can transfer people into a kind of ecstasy that expresses itself as a passion for suffering as a way of attaining union with God. But extreme and pathological masochism has expressed itself more in ascetic than in mystical directions. The mystics' question remains how people can come to accept grief as joy. Thus it is not the theodicy question, whether God wants to punish the sufferers or whether he has forgotten them or whether he loves them in spite of their suffering—or precisely because of it. Even the way of putting the question is no longer how a child would put it, Do you love even me? but an adult, How can people put their love for God into practice? "Even their affliction must be pure sugar for those who love God," says Johann Franck, which is similar to Tauler's idea that a person becomes capable of laying hold of "love in suffering, sweetness in what is sour." The question is whether the "love-power," the will, can lead people to such a transforming kind of suffering.

Mystical theology arose under the monstrous weight of suffering in the late Middle Ages and mirrors the helplessness of people in their woes and their protests against them. The institutions they had inherited had nothing to say to people. "Go to God yourself" is an admonition from the fourteenth century that contains a pointed attack against ecclesiastical regimentation and sacramentalism. What is now commended is "our Lord's suffering, the use of which is free, since neither pope nor priest can forbid it."[10]

Heretical lay movements were the breeding grounds for

10. Albert Auer, *Leidenstheologie des Mittelalters* (Salzburg: Igonta-Verlag, 1947).

such theology. Even the use of the German language was a subversive act. The papal bull of excommunication against Eckhart makes the point that "he gave talks in front of the common people, which in itself is sufficient to obscure the true faith" and that his teaching would have to be uprooted, "so that it doesn't poison the hearts of the simple any further." The political consequences were drawn by the pupils of Eckhart and Tauler, the revolutionary Baptists, the Hussites, Thomas Müntzer in the peasants' war. "A subject who thought himself to be in personal union with the Lord of Lords provided, when things got serious, a very poor example indeed of serfhood."[11]

The traditional theological theories were no longer adequate. In them, indeed, suffering is incorporated in an Augustinian-Platonic way, so that the suffering recedes behind the good one can gain from it. That would still be the "business spirit" of which Eckhart speaks. Whoever wants goods rather than the good, whoever wants the gifts of God rather than God, whoever acts with the question, What's in it for me? always in mind, he is a merchant over against God, he uses his behavior to bargain with God. For him reality is only a means to predetermined ends, and in this way it loses precisely the character of reality. And God, who gives gladly and freely, is missed in such calculation. Eckhart's ethic is a doctrine about acting without asking, What's in it for me? The new teachings about suffering are no longer fed by the theological *summae,* such as that of Thomas Aquinas, but by two other sources: first, the consolatories, which take up the ideas coming from stoicism; and secondly, the mystical currents which answer the question, "Why does God treat his friends so badly in this age?"

In mysticism, suffering is the object of burning love. "I say that next to God there is no nobler thing than suffering

11. Bloch, op. cit., p. 65.

... [and] God is always with a man in suffering. ... "[12] Compared with the passion of this acceptance, every other theory about suffering is a "paltry, cold, haughty fencing posture."[13] It is reported that when suffering again struck Suso after a lengthy period he said, "God be praised! God has thought of me and not forgotten me."[14] Tauler tells about a priest who strove after God without a discipleship of suffering and without passing through Christ's humanity and who thereby was shattered.

Three stages in the mystical way can be distinguished in Tauler and Eckhart: from "suffering," by way of "dying to self," to "receptiveness to God." The first step, natural suffering, is evoked by clinging to finitude, the enjoyment of finite things *mit Eigenschaft* (with possessiveness), as Tauler and Eckhart say. The meaning of the Middle High German word *Eigenschaft* moves between our words "possession, peculiarity, characteristic, ownership." "To own something possessively" designates a self-centered possession of things, among which can be reckoned one's own achievements, even God. The person possesses things for himself and is therefore possessed by the things. Christ is the model for possession without "possessiveness": "Now take his ... blessed poverty; heaven and earth were his, and he never used them possessively" (Tauler).[15] From "using things possessively" grows everything that can injure the self: pain, care, disconsolateness, fear, and despair. Creaturely possession entails suffering, but only a passive kind, forced out of a person. Detachment from things enjoyed possessively, "sitting loose," dying to self, this is a painful process. It brings people into discontent, fear, and darkness. Yet this suffering "never has the passivity of a

---

12. *Eckhart*, op. cit., pp. 262f. (Sermon #104).
13. Auer, op. cit., p. 56.
14. Heinrich Seuse, *Deutsche mystische Schriften* (Düsseldorf: Patmos-Verlag, 1966), p. 92.
15. Cf. Christine Pleuser, *Die Benennungen und der Begriff des Leidens bei Johannes Tauler* (Berlin: Erich Schmidt Verlag, 1967), pp. 61, 56.

quietistic endurance."[16] Suffering is a form of change that a person experiences; it is a mode of becoming. According to scholastic thought becoming means, "in so far as it arises from an action—doing; in so far as it is included in something that is received—suffering." Tauler takes up these ideas. The being of God consists in giving being, the creature does nothing but receive being. "If two are to become one, they have to relate to one another in such a way that the one suffers and the other acts."[17] But this relationship between God and man as acting and suffering has been destroyed by original sin. Man, who "uses things possessively" can no longer "suffer." His reason is occupied with pictures of finitude, the "ground" of his soul is not "unoccupied." Therefore he must first "die to self" and become like nothingness. The more a person dies to self, "keeps himself in a state of suffering," the more receptive he is to the action of God. Suffering and letting go are set over against acting and having.[18]

It is important to make it clear that the contrast is not between activity and passivity. There is more "loving," more willing, to suffering and letting go than to the natural doing and possessing from which the purely worldly suffering of the first stage arises. What is to be learned is the letting go, from which follow calmness, remoteness of soul, poverty.

These forms of becoming free from bondage to everything "that takes away freedom" (Eckhart) lead to the stage of "receptiveness to God." Understood theologically receptiveness to God is the experience of God, the *cognitio dei experimentalis*. As the person emerges from bondage to things he is once more attuned to the action of God. The spirit can be "a pure suffering within itself," can assimilate God and become one with him.

16. Ibid., p. 73.
17. Ibid., p. 74.
18. Ibid., p. 75.

This mystical line of affirming suffering by becoming one with God remained in force in theologies of suffering only by means of compromises. The two directions that theologies of suffering were going—that of stoicism and of mysticism—converge. The *Zwölfmeisterlehre,* which contains examples of the mysticism found in cloisters in the fourteenth and fifteenth centuries, binds both tendencies together and determines the church's point of view until the Reformation. A person is to view suffering as a gift "that one true friend gives another." Love for the cross and stoic *ataraxy,* the virtue of tranquility, become mixed with one another, to the detriment of both.

TRANQUILITY AND LOVE OF THE CROSS

A compromise between the stoic and Christian-mystical concepts of suffering is actually impossible. One needs to compare the artistic portrayals in Roman portraits with those out of the autumn of the Middle Ages in order to see the difference between stoic self-restricting tranquility and the "sweetness" of mystical suffering. One needs to compare the prosaic language of the consolatories from the Middle Ages, with their classification of various benefits and advantages that can attract the soul out of suffering, with the erotically tinted language of mystical texts in order to recognize the incompatibility of these two ways of arranging and conquering suffering. Of course, within western history there were attempts again and again to combine a stoic and a Christian interpretation, baroque tragedy offering perhaps the most significant example. But the starting and finishing points still remain incompatible. The stoic denies suffering and by a gesture of tranquility does not allow it to enter his soul. The consolatories of the Middle Ages are stoic and ascetic in orientation. Their ideal is the *senex sapiens,* "the wise old man," not the mystics' lover of God. With a prosaic matter-of-factness and harshness their instructions on how to overcome suffering present, on the one hand, possibilities for the avoidance of suffering and, on the other, use of unavoidable suffering. Stoicism in the Middle Ages is aware that a person's true happiness lies exclusively within, independent of outer circumstances and of Fortuna, the ancient goddess of joy, by now often viewed sarcastically and pessimistically. From Fortuna, from entrusting onself to her care, comes suffering; only by training oneself to achieve tranquility can a person secure a place to stand in the face of such suffering. What people call evil is only illusionary and does not touch the wise.

This spiritual line continues in the Renaissance and forms a "closed type of suffering theory," which inevitably stresses the ancient concept of fate.[19] The alternation of the rhythm of life entails suffering as something natural. The supernatural, that is, the understanding of suffering as something that produces change, recedes.

While in the language of mysticism "calmness" designates the frame of mind of a person who has renounced himself and all things and become free for God, the meaning of the word later shifts to the stoic concept of suffering: the source of calmness is no longer God but indifference; the absence of emotions brings people to a world-conquering coldness, which moves along with a tone of resignation.

The exterior and distorted form of this stance is apathy, which is incapable of suffering. The attempt to keep suffering from entering the soul is indeed only possible if it is a limited, for example, physical, suffering which has not reached the three-dimensionality of which Simone Weil speaks. The night of being abandoned by God is not experienced in this case; it is impossible to be forsaken by the God *Logos* (Reason).

A significant representative of this viewpoint in this century is the late Brecht. The suggestions he gives for dealing

19. Auer, op. cit., p. 48.

with suffering caused by political power all amount to making oneself small, untouchable, insensitive; only he who keeps everything at arm's length will survive. The ancient stoic advice to live in seclusion lingers on here. Tranquility unites with indifference and cunning at the same time. It saves itself for the day that is coming after the dark times of power.[20] Freud also approaches the stoic line in his understanding of suffering that cannot be averted. One can view his criticism of religion as a criticism of people's false and excessive expectations and desires. "Our God, Logos, will fulfill whichever of these wishes nature outside us allows. . . . He promises no compensation for us, who suffer grievously from life."[21] In contrast to the "illusion" which religion represents *Logos* and *Ananke* (Necessity) designate the true God. The acknowledgment of this God brings with it the endurance of suffering, which is seen as a necessary part of life.

Socially and politically expressed, tranquility is an ideal for the upper classes, just as the apathetic God is not the God of the little people and their pain. In stoic piety the present world and humanity within it are seen as good; indeed the world is seen as "Zeus' perfect city," so that any revolt must appear unthinkable, indeed absurd.

The Christian understanding of suffering, as it expresses itself in the mysticism of the cross, is different from this. Here the stance over against suffering is not that of averting or avoiding it. For the religion of slaves and of the poor, avoidance and "the hidden life" are not real possibilities. The mystical way points in the opposite direction: the soul is open to suffering, abandons itself to suffering, holds back nothing. It

20. Cf. Bertolt Brecht, "Massnahmen gegen die Gewalt," *Gesammelte Werke,* Vol. 12 (Frankfurt: Suhrkamp Verlag, 1967), p. 375.
21. Sigmund Freud, "The Future of an Illusion," *The Standard Edition of the Complete Psychological Works of Sigmund Freud,* trans. from the German under the general editorship of James Strachey, in collaboration with Anna Freud, assisted by Alix Strachey and Alan Tyson, Vol. 21 (London: Hogarth Press, 1961), p. 54.

does not make itself small and untouchable, distant and insensitive; it is affected by suffering in the fullest possible way. The extreme and distorted form of this stance is masochism. Its distortion consists in anticipating the pleasure that deliverance affords; the way is mistaken for the goal. But a true acceptance of suffering is never a self-sufficiency which would be at peace and satisfied already now in the devil's inn. The acceptance of suffering by giving oneself over to it rather than facing it with tranquility arises out of a different relationship to the future. The God who says, "Behold, I make all things new" (Rev. 21:5), cannot himself exist now without suffering over what is old. What is promised is not only a restoration of elemental goodness after the storm of power, but the abolition of all power by which some men dominate others, all anguish. That is why, in the Christian understanding of suffering, mysticism and revolution move so close to one another.

"For God only speaks in his creatures' proneness to suffering, which the hearts of unbelievers don't possess."[22] This "proneness to suffering," that is, the suffering that a person has experienced as well as the capacity to suffer, is what makes him stronger than anything that comes his way. What is meant is not only that it is better to suffer wrong than to do it, although this thought—with its rejection of the illusion of neutrality—does play a role in the Christian explanation of suffering. But what is decisive for Christian mysticism is first of all the knowledge that the one who suffers wrong is also stronger (not just morally better) than the one who does wrong. That "God is always with the one who is suffering" entails not only consolation but also strengthening: a rejection of every ideology of punishment, which was so useful for the cementing of privileges and for oppression. There is a mystical defiance that rebels against everything ordained and

22. Thomas Müntzer, "Das Prager Manifest, November 1521," *Die Fürstenpredigt. Theologisch-politische Schriften* (Stuttgart: Reclam, 1967), p. 8.

regulated from on high and holds fast to the truth it has discovered. "Not God himself, not angels, nor any sort of creature is able to separate from God the soul who is in the image of God."[23] That is the extension of Paul's thought: Nothing "can separate us from the love of God" (Rom. 8:39).

The Christian idea of the acceptance of suffering means something more than and different from what is expressed in the words "put up with, tolerate, bear." With these words the object, the suffering itself, remains unchanged. It is borne —as a burden, suffered—as an injustice; it is tolerated, although intolerable; borne, although unbearable. "Put up with" and "tolerate" point to stoic tranquility rather than to Christian acceptance. The word "take," also in its combination with "on, up, over," means that the person doing the accepting is himself changed. What I "take" belongs to me in a different sense from something I only bear. I receive a guest, agree to a proposal, take on an assignment; I say yes, I consent, I assent, I agree with.

THE AFFIRMATIVE IN CHRISTIANITY

This stance of acceptance is suspect in a two-fold way. With respect to the individual it can be taken as masochism, with respect to society as affirmation. It is "affirmative," serving to stabilize existing conditions; it is seen as a false reconciliation, a naive identification with that which "is," though it is in no sense very good. Isn't it only veiled submission, with all the social consequences that have attended Christianity's cult of suffering? For centuries this cult of suffering has been shamelessly exploited to justify injustice and oppression. Acceptance of suffering is an essential element in "piety," to use a key word for what is contained in the traditional concept of religion: "the pious attachment to the divine or the holy on the one side and on the other side its sociologically objective appear-

---

23. *Eckhart*, op. cit., p. 200 (Sermon #79—translation altered slightly).

ance."[24] The tendency to accept existing social and political realities stems from this piety. It is, of course, evident that this period of piety has come to an end, at least in regard to the acceptance of suffering. In this sphere piety no longer means submission, but insurance against suffering at almost any cost. It shows an absence of piety to be uninsured, to have taken no preventive actions, to have made no provisions for defense or for a place to hide.

Both objections to a Christian acceptance of suffering, that of masochism and that of affirmation, apply more readily to past than to present practice. Society, now free of religion and tending toward apathy, is more at home with affirmation than the residue of religious culture is able to be. Gone is the old connection between accepting personally experienced suffering and affirming social conditions which make suffering necessary. Today affirmation of existing conditions is not forced through suffering, and it needs no religious basis. Today all suffering, especially suffering that is obvious and not hidden, is a contradiction to the prevailing fashion. If the voice of religion in earlier times repeated, "Bear it patiently," today affirmation arises in entirely different places, where people are told that perpetual happiness is readily available. That is done completely in the interest of this prevailing fashion. Only when sorrow is suppressed and hidden can this kind of affirmation be maintained.

That applies also to seemingly radical formulations that, in the garb of enlightenment, recommend "abolition" as the answer to suffering. Then the slogan in respect to suffering is not "acceptance but abolition," as if the questions that suffering raises—even a single one of them—could be answered in that way! It is a kind of submission theology in reverse, only now the Lord who has given and who has taken away is

---

24. Cf. Heinze Robert Schlette, *Skeptische Religionsphilosophie. Zur Kritik der Pietät* (Freiburg: Verlag Rombach, 1972), pp. 147, 150.

no longer called God but the future society, and it promises: the Lord who has given will not afterwards take it away. Of course, it is necessary to relate every personal sorrow to society, that is, first to ask about its social causes, and then also to recognize that social conditions help determine the way in which suffering is endured and worked on. But that is not all that needs to be taken into account. If capitalism tries to make people believe that all affliction they encounter is their personal concern, their tough luck, to be endured by them, things are no different with a socialism that asserts the opposite. The concrete powerlessness then is left to those who today suffer wrongly in a distorted society. The expression "to abolish" takes suffering, which is an activity, an experience that people are involved in, and makes it a marketable commodity that one can acquire and get rid of.

Bazon Brock's provocative remark is to be understood in a similar way: "Death, that damned obscenity, must finally be abolished. Whoever speaks a word of comfort is a traitor." The substance of a thought of this kind is fascistic: death may no longer be interpreted, integrated, bemoaned, or surrounded by consolation. It must be removed from the realm of human experience. If it can be acquired, so it can also be abolished. And to accomplish this task of abolishing death, beyond the capacity of mere mortals, society looks to science. Then this god has the task of deciding who is worthy and unworthy of living.

Behind many of these considerations stand attempts to remove the problem of suffering from its global universality and to get a handle on it by dividing it in various possible ways. The most important of these distinctions is that between biologically derived and socially caused suffering. And these two categories are subdivided to distinguish between suffering that we can abolish and suffering we can at best soften. But as the case of the blinded Jacques Lusseyran clearly shows, the natural cause means virtually nothing compared with the social situation, on which the conquest even of natural and irreversible suffering decisively depends. Then all suffering would be dependent on the situation that people have created for one another and the share of purely natural suffering reduced to a minimum. That all suffering is social suffering, then, means that all suffering is to be worked on. No suffering can be clothed and transfigured any longer with the appearance of fate. But in that case it would also be unnecessary to rob natural suffering, precisely as purely natural, of its importance over against societal suffering that "can be abolished."

On the contrary, the help that a society gives to those who suffer from natural causes, for instance those who are incurably ill, is a measure of its humanity. The attempt at divisions becomes problematic when one believes he can distinguish "right" and "wrong" suffering. Certainly the suffering of the proletarian masses is objectively more important than that of a single artist. But this kind of "objectivity," applied consistently, destroys the capacity to perceive any suffering at all. Every unit can be relativized and minimized over against a greater whole. In the total span of world history sufferings evaporate as it is. It is a macabre spectacle to draw up a balance sheet that ranks people's sufferings in order of importance.

We should not make it easy for ourselves and wish to distinguish between right and wrong suffering, between proletarian and middle class suffering, between a child's affliction and that of a band of guerrillas, between that of an artist such as Kafka or Pavese and that of an insignificant salesgirl.

There is no wrong suffering. There is imaginary, sham, feigned, simulated, pretended suffering. But the assertion that someone suffers for the right or wrong reason presupposes a divine, all-penetrating judgment able to distinguish historically obsolete forms of suffering from those in our time, instead of leaving this decision to the sufferers themselves. Even the pain of children which can easily be alleviated is suffering that is neither right nor wrong. The division into meaningless and potentially meaningful suffering seems to me to come closest to reality. There is meaningless suffering on which people can no longer work, since it has destroyed all their essential powers.

Following an idea of Paul Tillich's, I would like to distinguish this meaningless suffering from suffering that can be meaningful since it impels one to act and thereby produces change. Christianity demands, says Tillich, "that one accept suffering with courage as an element of finitude and affirm finitude in spite of the suffering that accompanies it."[25] It is clear that Christianity makes an overwhelming affirmation of suffering, far stronger than many other world views that do not have as their center the symbol of the cross. But this affirmation is only part of the great love for life as a whole that Christians express with the word "believe." To be able to believe means to say yes to this life, to this finitude, to work on it and hold it open for the promised future.

"Not to accept an event which happens in the world is to wish that the world did not exist."[26] This statement of Simone Weil's sounds extreme, but it expresses with precision the sin of despair by which radical and unconditional affirmation of reality is destroyed. Suffering can bring us to the point of wishing that the world did not exist, of believing that nonbeing is better than being. It can make us despair and destroy our capacity for affirmation. We then cease loving God.

25. Paul Tillich, *Systematische Theologie*, Vol. 2 (Stuttgart: Evangelisches Verlagswerk, 1958), p. 80. [The translation follows the German edition of Tillich since the English makes a somewhat different point: *Systematic Theology*, Vol. 2 (Chicago: University of Chicago Press, 1957), p. 70].
26. Simone Weil, *Gravity and Grace*, with an Introduction by Gustave Thibon, trans. Arthur Wills (New York: G. P. Putnam's Sons, 1952), p. 197. Copyright © 1952 by G. P. Putnam's Sons. Reprinted by permission.

"To wish that the world did not exist is to wish that I, just as I am, may be everything."[27] This wish is the state of sin. The person is curved in upon himself; pain has caused introversion. He has no future and can no longer love anything. He himself is everything; that is, he is dead. To be able to live we need affirmation:

> Almost all have called the world their friend
> Before they get their handful of earth in the end.[28]

In this sense Christianity actually has an "affirmative" core; just as people who dare to bring a child into this world are acting "affirmatively." To put it in Christian terms, the affirmation of suffering is part of the great yes to life as a whole and not, as it sometimes can appear, the sole and the decisive affirmation, behind which the affirmation of life disappears entirely. The Bible speaks about God as the "lover of life" (Wisd. of Sol. 11:26) and in this way expresses an unending affirmation of reality. Jesus of Nazareth lived this unending affirmation. He drew to himself precisely those who lived on the fringes or were cast out, like women and children, prostitutes and collaborators. He affirmed those who were everywhere rejected and compelled to reject themselves. It is from the background of this affirmation of life, even the life of those who were sick, disabled, or too weak to accomplish much, that one must see the understanding of the acceptance of suffering as it developed in Christianity. It is an attempt to see life as a whole as meaningful and to shape it as happiness. It is an eternal affirmation of temporal reality. The God who is the lover of life does not desire the suffering of people, not even as a pedagogical device, but instead their happiness.

27. Ibid.
28. Bertolt Brecht, *Manual of Piety* or *Die Hauspostille*, trans. Eric Bentley, notes by Hugo Schmidt (New York: Grove Press, 1966), p. 93.

JOB IS STRONGER THAN GOD

Acceptance could still be understood as submitting ourselves to what we cannot change, what is stronger than we are. But instead of this, what is intended is a conquest, from which we come out defeated and at the same time stronger. Lusseyran lost his eyes and found the light. Acceptance does not mean that the blind are to remain blind. Getting free of existing suffering is the greatest theme of the Bible, an exodus out of oppression and forcibly imposed labor, out of collectively experienced suffering, arbitrarily imposed by rulers. The suffering of the children of Israel in Egypt is subjected in scripture to no theological interpretation. It is not ascribed to the will of an almighty God. On the contrary, it is Pharaoh who is almighty and blindly arbitrary, appointing taskmasters and increasing the production demands. The form of oppression is the enforced labor of slaves in construction and work in the fields; "in all their work they made them serve with rigor" (Exod. 1:14).

Thus the suffering of the people is not explained and toned down with the aid of ideas about punishment or testing or transformed into submissiveness. The suffering is there: blind, tyrannical, absurd. It befalls the entire nation, and the entire nation is led out. The God of the exodus is not one who imposes affliction and then, with equal arbitrariness, removes it again. The affliction is explained completely in rational terms. It stems from force employed by the Egyptians, who fear being supplanted by the ever-increasing numbers of Israelites. God has nothing to do with this suffering— aside from being on the side of the wronged.

The second great story about suffering in the Old Testament is different. It concerns an individual who lives in a legendary land and enjoys legendary good fortune. God allows this guiltless, God-fearing man to be tormented to the limit. The experiences that Job has are not unlike those of the people in Egypt, since extreme suffering and times of despair are similar to one another. Thus Job compares his suffering with that of "a slave, who longs for the shadow and . . . a hireling who looks for his wages" (Job 7:2). But God is no longer on the side of the slaves, the unfortunate, and the wronged; in this book he plays a different role.

This role is ambiguous, the author assigning a variety of roles to God. In the folktale about Job, the prologue and epilogue that frame the rest of the book, God is the tester who imposes certain limits on Satan but nevertheless consents to the experiment. God is thus one who tries people in order to prove them, who tests them not for a specific task but for the life of righteousness, for salvation.

The test, the trial, the experiment with a person's loyalty, veracity, and righteousness is a motif that is applied to a tyrannical ruler in the whole of early literature. Ancient mythology, and fairy tales as well, are full of stories in which an absolutely superior being suggests a test to someone small and weak, perhaps a contest, perhaps the imposition of tasks impossible of fulfillment. The sphinx at the gates of Thebes proposes riddles; the giant challenges the valiant little tailor to squeeze water from a rock; the shepherd boy may marry the princess, instead of being beheaded, if he drinks up an ocean or in a single night moves a palace from one place to another; the king in Rumpelstiltskin commands the poor miller's daughter to spin straw into gold. These kings, lords, and giants in fairy tales are despots who set the conditions of the contest in such a way that no human being can hope to fulfill them. Frequently, if the person being tested fulfills all that was required, the tester then devises still other, more difficult stipulations. In some fairy tales it goes so far that the one who has fulfilled everything, only to be cheated out of what is rightfully his, cuts off the king's head.

In the contests that belong to a more vacillating later phase of this development, the conditions are relatively fair, so that cunning and wit are sufficient to fulfill them: the little tailor squeezes water from a cheese, Jack sticks the pudding he can no longer eat into a sack. The true tests, on the other hand, are put in such a way that the mighty one himself could not fulfill them. All the greater, then, the triumph when the little one passes the test, aided by animals, spirits, or a magic charm. All creation, often even sun, moon, and stars, are bidden to help the weak against the superior one. If the test is passed, the mighty one loses the right to set up such tests.

It proved to be a case of might makes right. The experiment with man was thwarted by the man himself. Mythology does not express these thoughts abstractly, in the way Kant declares all conduct immoral that makes of another a means instead of an end. Mythology convicts the testers themselves of evil. They are stripped of power when the test is passed, contrary to the expectation and desire of the tyrant. This is only possible, however, for an absolutely "pure," single-minded being who does not fear death. The test-god can be stripped of his power only by one who is prepared to sacrifice himself or—since this way of putting it still sounds too heroic-moralistic—who goes to the test weaponless and guiltless, solely with the consciousness of his indestructibility.

The tests that Job has to endure are no less absurd and gruesome. Here too what is demanded is impossible of human fulfillment; the tester himself could never do it. The despot dictates the conditions of the contest. Job repeatedly suggests other conditions, but these are not accepted. Job is subjected to an experiment just as the prisoners in German concentration camps were subjected to medical experiments. Moreover, in their case there was even the stipulation that those who, contrary to expectation, survived stayed alive temporarily.

In one respect Job's test is different from the tests described in the myths, namely, in the substance of the demands. In the fairy tales it is the accomplishment of certain feats, while with Job it is human pain that is the theme of the testing. The distinctive element in the poem about Job is precisely that the realistic theme of suffering is combined with the motif of the tyrannical tester.

How does Job react to the testing? One needs to distinguish here between the old folktale, written in prose, and the appreciably more recent poem encased in the prose framework. In the folktale Job holds firmly to his piety, for which his wife reproaches him. It is actually the affirmative power in Job. He rejects the obvious advice: "Curse God and die!" He does not kill himself. Rather he suffers, he stands, he complains, he battles. The successful conclusion of the matter confirms that Job was not renounced by God. He withstood the test.

The situation is different in the poem. It is true that what could signify cursing God or renouncing him is not expressed here. But that is not because of the piety which the folktale ascribes to Job, which has made him in the entire eastern world into "the patient sufferer," thanks to whom even the camel has the name *abu Iyyub,* Father Job. The Job in the poem goes beyond simple forms of renunciation: he refuses to allow himself to be made the object of testing. Job is stronger than God. Job does what the fairy tale hero does only after he has passed the test. He disposes of the tester in the course of the testing itself:

Let me alone, for my days are a breath. What is man, . . . that thou dost set thy mind upon him, dost visit him every morning, and test him every moment? (Job 7:16b–18)

The passage from the Psalms that is used here sarcastically says the exact opposite. The psalmist is extolling the greatness of man, whom God made little lower than the angels (Ps. 8:5f.). Job takes God at his own words, which present men as lords over creation, as the crown of creation, and confronts these words with reality. In truth he is a defenseless object of the tester, a "target" (Job 7:20) for the "arrows" full of poison (6:4). The tyrannical character of God appears in a series of pictures: God hunts man as a lion hunts game (10:16); he imposes forced labor upon him as Pharaoh once did in Egypt; he is the one who drives the prisoners on, the master over slaves (3:18f.). His actions are described with words like: "oppress" (10:3), "despise" (10:3), "destroy" (10:8), "slash open" (16:13), "imprison," "deceive," "make fools of" (12:14 ff.); it is he who "prevails against" man and changes "his countenance" (14:20).

A testing of this kind can come only from an arbitrary tyrant. The senselessness of the testing is clear right from the start. The God who knows everything also knows that Job is blameless (10:6f.) and doesn't need to investigate that.

Job won't have anything to do with the tyrannical type of testing in which the powerful one dictates the conditions to the powerless. Contrary to the game God is playing with him, he insists on his rights and demands justice. The God of the exodus spoke with Moses "as a man speaks with his friend" (Exod. 33:11). Job insists on the same right; it is denied him.

The second possible role is assigned God by Job's friends, who try to make this God believable to Job himself. It is this God who punishes, who avenges people's offenses relentlessly. The friends, much like Calvin, think suffering has to be traced to sin: "Think now, who that was innocent ever perished? Or where were the upright cut off?" and, going on directly with intolerable naiveté, "As I have seen, those who plow iniquity and sow trouble reap the same" (Job 4:7f.).

They are certain that God, in keeping with his righteousness, will not reject a blameless man (8:20). Accordingly, suf-

113

fering has to be traced to evil on the person's part. When this is not visible one must search for it—within himself through self-examination or with the aid of others. But it is precisely his innocence that Job refuses to be talked out of. He insists on taking up a lawsuit with God in which his innocence would become evident. At the same time he knows it is senseless to assume that God would abide by the just judgment: "I shall be condemned; why then do I labor in vain?" And, in one of the pictures that shows the whole extent of affliction that turns inward and makes the person loathsome to himself: "Though I wash myself with soap or cleanse my hands with lye, thou wilt thrust me into the mud and my clothes will make me loathsome" (9:30f., NEB). In Job's view God is he who destroys the blameless like the wicked (9:22); in the face of that, the knowledge of being right (13:18) means nothing. God's essence is "power" and not "justice"; he bends justice and rules with raw power (19:6f.).

Actually the doctrine about the punitive nature of suffering, after the unequivocality of this rejection, needs to be silenced forever. It is almost incomprehensible that it has survived and been renewed again and again through the centuries within the framework of the same culture which produced the poem about Job. Job's friends don't die out!

The simplest explanation for that seems to be the phenomenon observed by Simone Weil, that people by nature respond to affliction as hens who rush upon a wounded hen with slashing beaks. Everybody "despises the afflicted to some extent, although practically no one is conscious of it."[29]

The idea of suffering as punishment is only the theological expression of this contempt. In the form in which it emerges

29. Simone Weil, "The Love of God and Affliction," *Waiting For God*, trans. Emma Craufurd with an introduction by Leslie A. Fiedler (New York: G. P. Putnam's Sons, 1951), p. 122. Copyright © 1951 by G. P. Putnam's Sons. Reprinted by permission.

through Job's friends it has lost every element of truth, namely, the function of threatened punishment that comes out of the prophetic tradition. But in that tradition the threat does not come in like an oracle, stated absolutely, but remains dependent on the behavior of the one who receives the threat. But here all that remains is the stupidly repeated: suffering is punishment for guilt. Elihu has the audacity to express a downright sadistic wish: "Would that Job were tried to the end, because he answers like wicked men" (34:36, RSV). Thus the "friends" turn out to be friends of the sorrow-producer rather than the victim. That corresponds to various instincts: of protection, of setting boundaries, of fear of contagion or defilement—which are, after all, laws of our faculties of perception to which the one suffering affliction is subject as well as the observers. "In the case of someone in affliction, all the scorn, revulsion, and hatred are turned inward. They penetrate to the center of the soul. . . . "[30] It is for that reason that Job asserts his innocence with such cries of despair, "it is because he himself is beginning not to believe in it; it is because his soul within him is taking the side of his friends."[31] In suffering the awareness of innocence becomes "an abstract, lifeless memory."[32]

In reports from those who are interrogated and tortured over a long period of time there are similar experiences of self-destruction, self-hatred, and loathing. Affliction defiles everything a person is. God would once again "thrust [Job] into the mud" (9:31, NEB). Accordingly "compassion for the afflicted is an impossibility. When it is really found we have a more astonishing miracle than walking on water, healing the sick, or even raising the dead."[33] In that context one must

30. Ibid.
31. Ibid., p. 121.
32. Ibid., p. 122.
33. Ibid., p. 120.

consider the experiences that Simone Weil had as a factory worker in the thirties. She understood the *condition ouvriere* (working conditions) as the condition of Job.

Job can no longer hope to engage God in a lawsuit. As in the political purges of the twentieth century, Job does not have in hand the "indictment" written by his adversary (31:35). God has "taken away his rights" (27:2). He does not complain only for himself; rather he raises the old question why things go so well for the wicked (21:7). But now he sharpens it and raises it anew as the theodicy question: Why does the Almighty allow evil (24:12)? Why does he look on without intervening while the oppressed and exploited suffer?

This question was not raised in "Israel's bridal period." The God of the exodus was himself the answer to the experience of oppression. But once the question is radically raised, no answer can be given within the context of an understanding of God that combines justice and omnipotence. Job is stronger than God: Job's thinking has to lead to atheism, for moral reasons.

But in addition to the role of the just punisher, God is assigned still a third role in the book of Job. Even the friends mix the case for punishment, which after all presupposes insight into guilt that has been incurred, with the case for pure submission. In the face of God's absolute purity, a human being cannot be "pure" (4:17). God puts no trust even in his angels and servants (4:18; 15:15), not even the sun and moon are "pure" (25:5)—how then a human being, who is appropriately called "maggot" and "worm" (25:6)! The call for submission stands thus in a context of anthropological pessimism not exactly illumined by the gospel. Thus the mildly clerical Eliphas offers Job fatherly advice:

Agree with God, and be at peace [with the one whom Job had earlier called a murderer, who kills the blameless like the wicked! 9:22]. . . . Receive instruction from his mouth. . . . If you return

to the Almighty and humble yourself, if you remove unrighteous-
ness far from your tents, . . . then you will delight yourself in the
Almighty (22:21ff.).

Job is advised: with eyes cast down, to pray; and, quite openly
in the speeches of Elihu, to "obey and serve him" (36:11). In
the speeches of the friends the brutal might is still cloaked
through God's justice, which is presupposed and emphasized.
But in the answers God himself finally gives Job, justice no
longer plays any essential role. The answers are on a completely different level, that of nature.

"Where were you when I laid the earth's foundations?"
(38:4, NEB), God asks Job, and then, in seventy further questions from the realm of the wonders of nature, offers him an
impressive demonstration of the power of the creator and
man's total insignificance. Side by side with examples from
cosmogony appear crude and senseless examples from the animal world—and even if the hymns about Behemoth, the hip-
popotamus, and Leviathan, the sea monster, are later inser-
tions, they fit very well into the picture of this God, who
wrapped the ocean in swaddling clothes as it came out of its
mother's womb (38:8f.), who sends dew and lightning and
binds the cluster of the Pleiades (38:31), but who knows no
answer to human suffering other than that of submission.
What is man, compared to oceans and galaxies, to impressive
meteorological displays, to the permanency of nature! A non-
entity, a grain of sand, a being that simply because of his
insignificance, his cosmic triviality, has no rights whatsoever.

This God is a nature demon, who bears no relation to the
God of the exodus and of the prophets. What once revealed
God to the prophets was not the depths of the sea but justice,
which flows like water. Even the God of the creation stories,
with their unambiguous theology about man, about the
human kingdom, will find nothing of interest here. That

117

Job at the conclusion of the book submits himself to this power-being who dwells beyond good and evil, is incredible because it is intolerable. Ernst Bloch tries to understand the thunderstorm which ends with Job's conformity as "a cover for the heresy Job so fearlessly wanted to proclaim."[34]

But then the question arises about another, a fourth interpretation of God, which takes seriously Job's revolt, his rebellion (23:2), and is developed from it. This interpretation is tied to a contested passage with a corrupt text in which Job speaks of the *goel* as a witness to his innocence and his rescuer from guilt (19:25). The word *goel,* which has traditionally been translated with *redemptor,* redeemer, means "advocate," or, more archaically, "blood-avenger." Against God the Murderer, who violates justice, Job appeals to another God. "O earth, cover not my blood, and let my cry find no resting place. Even now, behold, my witness is in heaven, and he that vouches for me is on high" (16:18f.). This passage is still surpassed by the one about the blood-avenger who still lives, about the witness of Job's innocence and his rescuer from guilt, whom Job will see with his own eyes (19:25ff.). This helper, this true friend, goes beyond all the roles for God offered in the book of Job. He is neither the arbitrary tester, nor the avenger who establishes his absolute purity by dirtying his own hands with blood, nor the Lord of stars, seas, and clouds, "the mere *Tremendum* of nature."[35] Following Bloch's interpretation one must observe here, as the opposite of all theodicy, "the exodus of man from Yahweh."[36] Job relies on the God who led his people out of suffering in Egypt. The God whom he encounters is merely another Pharaoh. "Job is pious precisely because he does *not* believe,"[37] which

34. Bloch, op. cit., p. 113.
35. Ibid., p. 116.
36. Ibid., p. 118.
37. Ibid., p. 122.

in the context can only mean, does not submit himself, but continues to wait for another.

But then Job's call for the advocate, the redeemer, the blood-avenger and blood-satisfier is to be understood only as the unanswered cry of the pre-Christian world which finds its answer in Christ. Job is stronger than the old God. Not the one who causes suffering but only the one who suffers can answer Job. Not the hunter but the quarry.

5

Suffering and Learning

With God nothing is impossible ... as we all must experience and comprehend when we come to faith, that we fleshly, earthly people should become gods through the incarnation of Christ and thus with him be God's disciples, taught and deified by himself, yes, indeed, much more, in him thoroughly changed, so that earthly life changes into heaven.[1]

A FOLKSONG FROM CHILE

At the beginning of this century the exploitation of Chile through British imperialism reached unbelievable proportions. The workers in the nitrate mines in the North were paid not with cash but with vouchers that could only be exchanged for provisions at the company stores. They worked sixteen or more hours every day. Sedition was met with harsh punishment. In December 1907 the first mass demonstration took place. Twenty to thirty thousand workers demanded justice. This peaceful demonstration by laborers and by children was suppressed with force. In the afternoon of De-

1. Thomas Müntzer.

cember 21, 1907, there occurred in Iquique one of the bloodiest massacres anyone in Latin America can recall. Three and a half thousand people were locked in an empty school and murdered. In 1971, in the sixth month of the democracy, a film appeared about "Santa Maria de Iquique." While being interviewed one of the survivors told of his experiences.

How and why did the strike occur? There were no houses for people then; only houses for rats, for lizards, for vermin, for the settlement was not planned for people but only for dogs and savages, which is exactly what the owners of the nitrate mines were. Comrade Recabarren asked us how long we wanted to continue to put up with exploitation by these emigrant pigs who had come to Chile to enrich themselves. But the real culprits were the managers who acted with their backing. They would have to stop the exploitation. They were to blame that the poor "Pampino" (as the mineworkers in the North were called) had no underwear to put on. Because of them there was no cash at all but only worthless vouchers. Then came that fatal day. They went to the Santa Lucia Mine, a column of people stretching perhaps 8, 10, 15, or even 20 blocks. Many had no more water. Many were hungry. The babies needed water. Little children fell down and couldn't go any further. For the sun burns more brightly there than here. The people assembled. Then a comrade spoke: "Mineworkers, we are the damned. These gentlemen owners of the nitrate mines lead a fine life and let their employees here pay for it. We are the damned, for we have to maintain this thankless bunch. Tomorrow we shall march to Iquique."

The committee led the way, the flags waving. An officer approached: Halt! Here is our petition! He took it and read our requests: We demanded an eight hour day, for in 1905 slavery began in Chile If we get no justice we shall appoint a committee to go to Santiago to speak with the government. For we demand only justice, not even a pay increase. He replied: "The president of the committee and his people have fifteen minutes to leave Santa Maria. Otherwise, everyone will be shot!" We already saw a cavalry regiment and an infantry regiment approaching. Here

a machine gun, one over there and in the rear three machine guns
with four men at each. And then they began to shoot. I still hear
the shots today. 3600 died, three thousand six hundred. . . .
After this massacre the following song arose in Chile:

One day there arose like a lament
that springs from the depths of the heart
and courses through the alleys of the camp
the cry of rebellion,
the pain in the breast of many,
the voice of revolt,
the cry for the rights of the working class.
Holy victims, who came from the pampas
with hope
and at their arrival heard only
the voice of machine guns,
the voice of these beasts,
who massacred without compassion,
drenched with the blood of the workers.
They are damned.
I demand revenge on those
who loaded the machine guns,
revenge for the sufferers who survive.
Revenge for the mineworkers who died at Iquique.
Dull were the faces
because of the times they had seen;
dark the hands from the nights of exploitation.
The hard fist of the people
breaks through shadow and silence
and voices summon to singing.
Come, comrade, fall in,
fall in in our unity.
Come, comrade, work along,
work along on your future.
Be on your guard,
and don't forget the night,
the shadows you vanquished.
Nothing will stop us,
nothing will stop us anymore.[2]

2. Text from "Santa Maria de Iquique," directed by and screen play by Claudio

The song speaks about suffering from experience. It contains what J. B. Metz has called "dangerous memory," memory of the victims and their tormentors. It is an example of the second phase of suffering; the sufferers have broken through "shadow" and "silence"; the faces grown "dull" and the hands made "dark" from exploitation, which recall the voiceless suffering of the first phase, have now changed. The lament "arises." The language of this suffering is psalmic: the wrong will not be forgotten, the dead are not dead, from the lament comes the accusation. The cry for revenge and retribution comes, as in the ancient Psalms, from the knowledge of one's own righteousness. Remembrance of what has been endured summons the future. Insight into the necessity of revolution arises in the song itself; the singing is itself the exodus out of the mute phase of numb pain. The song is an example of proletarian culture—no less than the Psalms or Greek tragedy—which asserts that man learns through suffering (*pathei manthanein*), experiences change, is directed toward wisdom.[3]

But in the experiences reflected in the song from Chile the possibility also exists that suffering can make one callous, bitter, insensitive, and mute. It is not self-evident, and not a simple result of economic repression, that out of suffering comes the cry of rebellion. What that takes is people who learn from

Sapiain (Dicap, Chile Films Santiago, 1971). Cf. also the text of a recent cantata from Chile in M. de los Milagros Verde and P. Landau, "Mit der Gitarre kämpfen, Chilenische Chansons," *Dokumente* (March 1973), pp. 53ff.

3. Cf. Aeschylus, *Agamemnon*, lines 176ff.:

> [Zeus] setting us on the road
> Made this a valid law—
>   "That men must learn by suffering."
> Drop by drop in sleep upon the heart
> Falls the laborious memory of pain,
> Against one's will comes wisdom;
> The grace of the gods is forced on us
>   Throned inviolably.

The Agamemnon of Aeschylus, trans. Louis MacNeice (New York: Harcourt, Brace and Co., n.d.), p. 19. Reprinted by permission of Faber and Faber Ltd.

suffering, who do not blunt or forget the pain. Political consciousness arises *"ex memoria passionis,* political action of the people from the remembrance of humanity's passion history."[4] Apart from the consciousness of the vanquished and the remembrance of the victims the "cry of rebellion" cannot arise. For the ones engaged in revolution this means that all suffering that does not destroy them teaches them to love life all the more; it teaches a greater readiness to act for change.

Suffering makes one more sensitive to the pain in the world. It can teach us to put forth a greater love for everything that exists. It is not decisive whether or not we ascribe to "God" this change that suffering effects; even this teacher is bound to his pupils. What is essential is whether we carry out the act of suffering or are acted upon, indifferent as stones. What matters is whether the suffering becomes our *passion,* in the deep double sense of that word. The act of suffering is then an exercise, an activity. We work with the suffering. We perceive, we express ourselves, we weep. To consider the tearless male as an ideal is to acknowledge clearly that nothing is learned from suffering and nothing to be gained from it. We bury or else we unearth what we have hidden within us; we throw off or else take on a burden in suffering; we conceal ourselves from others or else we exhibit ourselves to them. Our hopes can die or they can grow in suffering. The bitterest pill is that "learning from suffering" can come to naught. It has then turned out to be an illusion, that an illness improves, that a case will be decided justly, that a person gets rid of his fears, or that the abolition of private property ushers in the promised liberation of the means of production. All this can end in disappointment. Many people are overgrown with dead hopes like land overgrown with ghostlike flowers.

The Chilean workers who call to mind the story of their

4. J. B. Metz, "Erinnerung des Leidens als Kritik eines teleologisch-technologischen Zukunftsbegriffs," *Ev. Theologie* 4 (1972), p. 343.

own suffering transform the act of suffering into purposeful activity. The experience leads them to action. They overcame the massacre not by treating it as a "natural" event but by laying hold of it as part of their own history.

All suffering that strikes us takes on in its raw actuality the character of a natural event. The metaphors from the realm of nature that we use to speak about suffering—night, snow, hailstorm, dark, rain, storm, raging sea—not only call to mind earlier experiences of suffering but at the same time designate the unalterable character of the events themselves. When Simone Weil says that it is "natural" to despise the unfortunate, this must be expanded to include the contempt sufferers inflict on themselves, in that they understand the suffering that strikes them as natural and, apart from any attempt to work with the suffering, comprehend it as alien and senseless fate. Thus senseless suffering deprives us of the activity of living. It merely destroys, it does not alter.

But the cry coming in the midst of pain is already in itself a physical easing of pain, since the crest of the pain wave moves along with a form of activity, however slight, as it comes to expression in protesting, facial contortion, groaning, or screaming. But it is in the other dimensions of suffering (psychological and social) that activity and practice come into play all the more. Here traditional theology is quite correct to use metaphors from the realm of nature, insofar as they connect suffering with work, which serves in the conquest of nature. Metaphors such as "plowing under, digging up, grafting and refining" point to this connection. Even complaining is an example of working through suffering, and "learn to suffer without complaining" is bad advice. Nothing can be learned from suffering unless it is worked through.

As with all historical experiences there are various possibilities for relating oneself to suffering. We can remain the people we were before or we can change. We can adopt the attitude of the "knowing one," of the clever person who saw it coming, who says, "that's the way things have always been"; who won't allow himself to experience the horror of it all, who looks at the future in the same way—but we can also find our way to the other attitude, that of learning.

In a certain sense learning presupposes mystical acceptance: the acceptance of life, an indestructible hope. The mystics have described how a person could become free and open, so that God is born within the depths of his soul; they have pointed out that a person in suffering can become "calm" rather than apathetic, and that the capacity for love is strongest where it grows out of suffering. "God is with those who are suffering" doesn't signify what a child means when he is beaten up and says, "My big brother will get you!" It means that love, when it is possessed by those who are suffering, is more invulnerable and serene than in any other life situation. It has become more independent of the fulfillments that come from the outside; it is more unconditional. The sufferers have no more to lose at the hands of fate; they are through with the God who is understood as an alien being who controls everything. They have everything to gain, not as a gift given them from outside but as a change within themselves, the strength of the weak. Independence from the God who destines how the classes should be ordered is precisely the strength of those who sing about the suffering at Santa Maria de Iquique. "Blessed are those who mourn" means for them the consolation of liberation: all who learn in suffering, who use their experiences to overcome old insights, who experience their own strength and come to know the pain of the living in the realm of the dead, they are beginning the exodus.

THE BITTER CHRIST

But has Christianity anything at all to do with this "learning from suffering"? Wasn't its answer to suffering again and again merely to submit, as Job's friends require of him to this day? In the context of general societal apathy toward the suffering of others, submissiveness over against personally experienced suffering leads to insensibility. Far and wide, contemporary Christianity is the suffering-free religion for a world perceived as without suffering. It is the religion of the rich, the white, the industrial nations. Its God is a mild and apathetic being. In this religion suffering is shrunken down into a purely personal affair without general interest. For the great suffering upon which nations construct their prosperity occurs in other parts of the world, far outside our field of vision. This suffering is at the same time easy to fit into contexts that have nothing to do with us, too high a birth rate and inadequate industrialization, for example. In this way we cover the fact that our profit is made from the suffering of others. The world of the rich, sealed air-tight against hunger and disease, doesn't need to devote any special attention to the problem of suffering even in its own midst. This inner apathy is in accord with the political and economic situation. Exploitation needs a certain amount of apathy in order to run its course smoothly.

This situation is expressed theologically in the teaching that what Christ has done for us is sufficient, so that our suffering is no longer necessary for the realization of salvation. If one understands salvation in an individualistic sense, then this teaching is totally logical. Since in this case the kingdom of God and the realization of righteousness do not mean, first of all, salvation for everyone, the redemption of the individual is not dependent on his deeds or his sufferings, which are also construed as works. Then the actual suffering that still strikes us is bereft of any supernatural, any spiritual quality. It no longer has the task of "leading us to wisdom" or bringing us to learning; it is downgraded into a natural evil and stripped of importance. In the context of such a perfectionistic theology suffering is meaningless for our liberation. This suffering-free religion was criticized in passionate language already at its inception at the beginning of the Reformation era, because it preached "a honey-sweet Christ, quite congenial to our murderous nature."[5]

Thomas Müntzer introduced the distinction between the bitter and the honey-sweet Christ in order to express his criticism of a suffering-free Christianity as he saw it set forth in Luther's Reformation. The doctrine of the sweet Christ asserts that all suffering has already been "accomplished," in Christ it is already finished. He has done everything for us; we need only "charge it to Christ's account"; faith is the acceptance of this completed salvation, ready and waiting for us. This faith, "that suffering is put on Christ alone, as though we are not permitted to suffer," corresponds politically to the two kingdoms doctrine, ecclesiastically to infant baptism.

The God of this "imaginary, unexperienced, untested" faith is none other than the heathen God, the God of apathy. According to the Koran, God didn't allow Jesus to go to the cross because he was "much too gentle for that"; he put someone else, an evildoer, in Christ's place, and only the unsuspecting Christians were deceived. Müntzer uses this conception of God from the Koran in order to polemicize against a suffering-free Christianity that stems from the same "incredibly carnal spirit." The apathetic God is "an immovable God"[6] who is a stranger to suffering. He can only be thought of along with the sweet Christ; his teaching is accepted without changing people. The way the world is governed remains untouched by this teaching. Humanity's suffering is not taken seriously. But "whoever does not want the bitter Christ will eat himself to death on honey."[7]

The bitter Christ is experienced in a discipleship of suffer-

---

5. Thomas Müntzer, *Die Fürstenpredigt. Theologisch-politische Schriften* (Stuttgart: Reclam, 1967), p. 38.
6. Ibid., p. 35.
7. Ibid., p. 22.

ing. Suffering, not just believing, is the way to God. No one will be with God "until he has overcome through his suffering (which is his lot perpetually)."[8] First one must endure hell; all other ways, "which bring consolation before affliction," bring a faith that is merely received outwardly. The bitter Christ means that we "let God uproot the thorns and thistles" that are in us. The cheap grace spoken of by Bonhoeffer is already attacked here, the idea that people could "so easily come to faith in Christ, if they only think about what Christ has said. No, my dear fellow, you must endure and know how God himself uproots the weeds, thistles and thorns out of your fruitful land, that is, out of your heart." By trusting the "sweet Christ," a person wants "to be in the image of God so that he no longer wants, does not even completely desire to attain the image of Christ."[9] To want to be in the image of God signifies a way without suffering, without fear. Faith remains unexperienced. It is merely received outwardly. To be in the image of God without attaining the image of Christ is a suffering-free Christianity—which, however, means at the same time one that leaves suffering to others. Bourgeois Christianity, as it was set forth as a result of Luther's teaching, is criticized here at the beginning of the Reformation with a sharpness and radicality that reminds one of Kierkegaard.

The desire to attain the image of God without going the way of Christ can be explained in various ways. First, it could stem from the conviction that Christ has indeed done everything for us, so that in his suffering and dying everything has been paid in full. What one suffers now still, in the history after the fact, history's postlude, so to speak, is to be patiently endured as insignificant. An *imitatio Christi* contradicts such a faith. In Luther's thinking that comes under works and attempts to attain salvation through one's own efforts. Luther's

8. Ibid., p. 23.
9. Ibid., p. 21.

Good Friday sermons are full of the fear that someone could "mix up" Jesus' suffering and ours.[10] But that means an end to the worth that human suffering had as an extension or completion of Christ's sufferings. The assertion that in Christ everything has been fulfilled remains in that case completely without content, an ideal of lordship that excludes us.

But there are also modern forms of the desire to attain the image of God apart from the image of Christ. In various forms of the current theology of hope, fulfillment is tied to God's (future) action. It is God who frees, who acts, and in the exuberance of hope the motif of the freeing God of the future comes to the fore much more strongly than the messianic suffering in the tradition, which tied fulfillment to "the woes" and salvation to suffering and learning. In this case God's triumph dominates the scene and people who suffer now can only fit themselves into the picture as later recipients, as participants, and yet not the kind of participants from whose own pain the new is erected. To say it in another way: the desire to be in God's image without attaining Christ's image is a desire for immediacy, which wants everything without detour and without self-actualization, a narcissistic desire of the ego to settle down in God, immortal and almighty, that doesn't find it necessary "to let its life be crucified" and to experience the night of pain. To meditate on the cross means to say good-bye to the narcissistic hope of being free of sickness, deformity, and death. Then all the energies wasted on such hopes could become free to answer the call for the battle against suffering.

To want to be in God's image without attaining Christ's image means in our world worshiping the great Pharaoh. No

---

10. Cf., for instance, Martin Luther, *Luthers Werke in Auswahl*, Vol. 7, *Predigten* (Berlin: De Gruyter, 1950), p. 102: *et non menge ineinander tuam passionem et Christi* (and do not mix with one another your suffering and Christ's), and p. 103: *ne misceas tuam passionem passioni Christi* (don't mix your suffering with the suffering of Christ).

longer is it carried out essentially in the form of submission to an incomprehensibly imposed fate. Religious submission is the idolatry of a time of deprivation, a time when privation breaks out anew in the most diverse places. In a time of plenty and of the alleviation of elementary needs for a part of humanity, Pharaoh, as the guarantor of this prosperity, no longer has to force people into submission. He has better methods to keep people from leaving and rebelling. Compulsion and force are unnecessary when persuasion and seduction do the job. Apathy replaces submission. It becomes everybody's number one priority at all costs to be among the suffering-free, who alone worship this Pharaoh properly, by producing more and consuming more, all the while denying the existence of unprevented pain.

To attain the image of Christ means to live in revolt against the great Pharaoh and to remain with the oppressed and the disadvantaged. It means to make their lot one's own. It is easy to be on Pharaoh's side if one just blinks an eye. It is easy to overlook the crosses by which we are surrounded. Naturally one can attempt to develop a theology that no longer has the somber cross at its center. Such an attempt deserves criticism not because it bids farewell to Christianity as it has been, but because it turns aside from reality, in the midst of which stands the cross.

But when Thomas Müntzer speaks of attaining the image of Christ and regards suffering as the way to get there, he does not mean all suffering. Neither the enforced renunciation and feudal labor of the peasants nor slaving away for one's masters is suffering that conforms a person to the image of Christ. The suffering necessary for a Christian, with its stages of anxiety, of "refining," of renouncing cravings that bind us to the world, of the sense of wonder which "begins when one is a child of six or seven years"—this way to Christ as a way of suffering is accessible only after the abolition of force and injustice which so enslave the poor man that he is unable to read the scriptures, that he is cut off from all possibilities for life. Suffering that conforms us to the image of Christ has nothing to do with the glorification of labor, of the peasants, for example, as it was articulated at that time against the early stages of the class of freemen in the cities. The bitter Christ does not put up with social suffering as such, does not preach tolerating it—so that goodness is not mixed with a toleration of injustice.

In his late manifesto to the miners in Allstedt, Müntzer made the distinction most clearly: "If you don't want to suffer for the sake of God, then you must become the devil's martyrs."[11] For him there is no neutral suffering, no suffering that remains "natural." Our only choice is for whose sake we suffer, not whether we have to suffer or remain free of suffering. With his phrase "the devil's martyrs," Müntzer is referring to the oppressed, extorted, exploited peasants who stay under the domination of their masters and tolerate them. The suffering of these non-revolutionary peasants is fruitless, without change. It can only stupify them or turn them into beasts. In the condition of oppression they are unable to be free from the fear of men. "A person cannot tell you anything about God as long as he rules over you."[12] The idea that the devil also has his martyrs, that is, that there is suffering that serves to strengthen his kingdom, sharpens anew the question about suffering. This distinction is not to be found in the substance of the suffering. It does not focus on the causes of the suffering but on its effect.

Müntzer distinguishes those who suffer for the devil's sake from those who in their suffering, by their pain, serve the pain of God. Thus Paul always distinguished godly grief from

---

11. Thomas Müntzer, "Manifest an die Allstedter Bergknappen," 15, cited from H. J. Schultz, ed., *Die Wahrheit der Ketzer* (Stuttgart: Kreuz-Verlag, 1968), p. 116.
12. Ibid., p. 117.

worldly grief according to the goal they served (2 Cor. 7:8–10). Paul spoke of the results of the grief that God willed the Corinthians to experience. They changed, they grew more autonomous: "For see what earnestness this godly grief has produced in you, what eagerness to clear yourselves, what indignation, what alarm, what longing, what zeal, what punishment!" (2 Cor. 7:11, RSV). In this way Paul circumscribes what we called the "practice" of suffering, which moves forward with passionate words and deeds. Worldly grief, on the other hand, can lead to death, that is, it can put people into a deathlike, unconnected condition of paralysis. The grief that God works conforms us more closely to Christ and makes us more alive, more capable both of pain and of love. This distinction between godly and worldly grief confirms everything we said about suffering and learning, about suffering and working. Moreover, people can transform even the suffering that appears to be a suffering unto death, even the bitter pain of destroyed hope, and turn it in the direction of life.

"I AND THE FATHER ARE ONE"

If the most important question addressed to suffering is whom it serves, God or the devil, becoming alive or paralysis, passion for life or the destruction of this passion, then the other question addressed to suffering, namely, that of theodicy, appears to be superceded. The almighty Lord, who ordains suffering or frees one from it has in that case lost his all-surpassing significance. Whoever grounds suffering in an almighty, alien One who ordains everything has to face the question of the justice of this God—and he must be shattered by it. Then all that remains is either total submission to God's omnipotence, together with a renunciation of the question about his justice, as Job did at the last, or else rebellion against this God and the awaiting of another deliverer. People who are shattered by this God experienced as heteronomous, who allows evil as if he were possessed by our baser instincts, are people who think too much of God and too little of themselves. Precisely under the veil of theism a thoroughly worldly grief arises, leading to unrelatedness.

Whom does suffering serve? What does it achieve? Many dream of a better world but are unable to integrate their personal suffering with the universal dream. But when this integration does occur, when people give their lives in hope for all, then other forms of suffering also appear. A testimony to this kind of suffering and dying is provided in the last letters of those condemned to death in the years 1939-45. It is important to preserve a memory of these letters also for the second half of the century—not because the same kind of fascism threatens us, but rather because this kind of suffering and learning, of dying and rising can help us.

A number of these letters remind us directly of Jesus' farewell discourses in the Gospel of John. They mirror a similar relationship to one's own suffering and dying and to those who are left behind. Both the writers of these letters and Jesus know that their death is unavoidable. The essential ingredient in these letters is not self-portrayals of pain and grief but concern for those who are left behind. "I will not leave you desolate; I will come to you. Yet a little while, and the world will see me no more, but you will see me; because I live, you will live also" (John 14:18f.). Jesus promises his friends peace. "In the world you have tribulation; but be of good cheer, I have overcome the world" (John 16:33). It was about the others that Jesus was anxious.

You imagine that a person condemned to die constantly dwells on it and regrets it. That's not true. From the beginning I thought about the possibility of death—as Verka well knows—and you have never observed any regret in me. I don't think about it at all. Death is always bad only for the living, for those who are left behind. Therefore I must wish you power and courage. I kiss and embrace you all till we meet again.[13]

Another writes his wife:

Alas! What can a person do who sits in prison under threat of certain death? And yet they are afraid of me. Tell the others. I know that I'm done for, and the sooner this moment comes the easier it is to endure. Farewell. I ask you to tell everyone that nothing is ended. I shall die, but you will live.[14]

As Jesus imparted peace to his friends and told them, "Let not your hearts be troubled, neither let them be afraid" (John 14:27), so also in these letters the request comes again and again: "Yet don't grieve. Others will spring up after my death, thousands."[15]

Believe me, nothing, nothing at all of what has happened has been able to touch the joy that is in me, a joy that announces its presence each day with a motif from Beethoven. They cannot make a person smaller by cutting off his head. And so, when everything has ended, I beg you from the bottom of my heart not to think of me with sorrow but with the joy with which I have always lived.[16]

This relationship between sorrow and joy is expressed again and again in the Gospel.

Truly, truly, I say to you, you will weep and lament, but the world will rejoice; you will be sorrowful, but your sorrow will turn into joy. When a woman is in travail she has sorrow, because her hour has come; but when she is delivered of the child, she no longer remembers the anguish, for joy that a child is born into the world (John 16:20f.).

13. *Letzte Briefe zum Tode Verurteilter aus dem europäischen Widerstand* (Stuttgart: dtv, 1962), p. 276.
14. Ibid., p. 306.
15. Ibid., p. 134.
16. Ibid., p. 278.

The letters from the resistance fighters also speak of this joy of having worked for the birth of a new world.

A second motif is their pride and their certainty that they have not lived in vain. Their life is not destroyed by death.

I don't want you to mourn for me. I want you to gather all your friends around the table and read them my letter and then drink to the repose of my soul. I don't want anyone to weep.[17]

Jesus spoke of completing his work, making known his Father's name (John 17:4, 6ff.), and of keeping and guarding his friends in the Father's name, so that they are not of the world: ". . . these things I speak in the world, that they may have my joy fulfilled in themselves" (John 17:13). The completion of his work through dying gives Jesus the right now to be himself glorified. The letter of a twenty-one-year-old resistance fighter bears the same certainty. "To everyone whom I love":

I am dying young, very young. There is something that will not die—my dream! Never has it been clearer, more splendid, closer to me than at this moment. Still, the hour of my sacrifice has come; the hour of its realization nears. My letter is coming to an end, the time is ending as well; only three hours separate me from death, my life is coming to an end.

Soon the harsh winter, soon the beautiful summer as well; I, I shall laugh about death for I shall not die. They will not kill me, they will bring me to eternal life. After my death my name will not sound like a death knell but like an upsurge of hope. Don't forget the imprisoned comrades whose families are without help.[18]

One can say about these people facing death that they were happier than their executioners. In their letters appears an almost painful sense of self-confidence, the superiority of those

17. Ibid., p. 132.
18. Ibid., p. 100.

who die for a just cause. But the attempt that Christian faith makes to assert that by his death Jesus became the Son of God means nothing else. The farewell discourses speak of a finally achieved certainty, of "glorification." The pride of those condemned to death stems from their prophetic self-assurance, an assurance of indestructibility. Happiness and freedom from fear belong to those whose names will not sound "like a death knell."

The court-martial has sentenced me to death. I'm writing these lines a few minutes before I die. I feel healthy, full of energy, full of boundless lust for life. . . . But there is no chance for rescue, I have to die. Yet I'm going to my death with inner strength and courage, as is fitting for people of our kind. I have lived 41 years, devoting 20 of them to the cause of the poor. All my life I have been an honest, faithful, tireless fighter, without personal interests. I was never deceitful. And as I have lived, so I die, since I know our cause is just and victory will be ours. The people will not forget me when better times come. One day history will record the truth, even about an insignificant person like me. I am dying and I shall live.[19]

The writer of these words is, like many others, a communist. His "I am dying and I shall live" has as its background no picture of the beyond after death, no expectation of continued individual existence. It is the paradoxical and precise expression about his life. Freedom from fear, certainty, strength, mark these letters. They grow out of participating in a cause that is greater than the people who work for it and die in the process. They know that their lives will conquer the death of being forgotten. "Thus I'm leaving you; stay well. Each one of you must now replace a century's worth of others."[20]

A third common motif is that many of the dying try to

19. Ibid., pp. 291f.
20. Ibid., p. 260.

impart a mission to those who remain. Just as Jesus again and again asked his disciples to love one another as he had loved them (John 13:34), to be for one another what he was for them, so also the ones who are dying hand on their own lives as a legacy, as a heritage entrusted to the survivors. These words were scrawled on the wall of a cell: "When this body is no more, this spirit will still live in the memory of those who remain behind. See to it that it is always an example." A daughter wrote her mother, "You must live and be brave so that, in my place, you can do much good in the world. I beg you, Mama."[21]

The certainty that comes from a death "freely given" (in the sense that it was brought about by one's own behavior), the concern for the survivors, the pride in one's own just cause and the ongoing task—these are traits that are just as characteristic of these letters as they are of Jesus' farewell discourses. The passion narratives are not objective accounts; rather they were written for our instruction. We recognize in them our opportunities to relate ourselves to the one enduring the blows and our own opportunities to suffer in a human way. An ancient prayer says, *passio Christi, conforta me* (Christ's suffering, strengthen me). How can that happen? Not simply in visualizing the suffering of Christ. This made sense in a time in which the divinity of Christ was self-evident and the suffering of Jesus could express God's participation in our suffering. The consolation that the passion offers us cannot be grounded in this presupposition. Not that the Son of God suffered, but how the man Jesus suffered means a strengthening, a presentation of human possibilities, a hope of humanizing even our suffering.

As pure history the story about Jesus has no overarching significance. It is only understood and appropriated when its continuation is understood. Jesus continues to die before our

21. Ibid., p. 283.

eyes; his death has not ended. He suffers wherever people are tormented. If we thought about Jesus' death only in a historical sense, without meditating on its ongoing nature, then this remembrance would remain a liturgy devoid of truth. In so far as we forget the continued dying of Jesus in the present we deny the passion itself. The injunction, "As often as you do this, do it in remembrance of me," overcomes forgetfulness and establishes a remembrance of Jesus' death which is only fulfilled when it is recognized in the victim's continuing death. The theological task is to hear the claim of Jesus in the farewell letters of the martyrs and to recognize his voice anew in their voices.

These people do not stand like children before an all-powerful father. To be sure they lament the loss of their life, but they no longer accuse a fate ruling over them. They don't ask, Why does God allow this? Even when they repeat, in other words, "My God, why have you forsaken me?" they maintain the certainty that Jesus expresses in the Johannine phrase, "I and the Father are one" (John 10:30). This certainty keeps them going: they know that they are "sent" to actualize justice, and their ongoing concern with justice means that they are "received up" in death, that they become "glorified." They are stronger than "the world" that triumphs over them.

Human suffering can be endured in this oneness with the Father that Jesus puts into words, in the indestructible certainty of the truth of a life lived for, and not against, humanity. Jesus' passion is the quintessence of such freely chosen suffering. It is suffering at the hands of the "world," of society that refuses to acknowledge Jesus' claim. It is also passion in the modern sense, passionate commitment to the unconditional. Like the saints, those condemned to death show us what it means to be able to endure the passion.

By nature suffering hits us in such a way that it makes us "the devil's martyrs." Fear, speechlessness, aggression, and blind hate are confirmed and spread through suffering. In Christ, that is, in humanity's true possibility, which is by no means self-evident, suffering summons our self-confidence, our boldness, our strength. Our oneness with love is indissoluble. To learn to suffer without becoming the devil's martyrs means to live conscious of our oneness with the whole of life. Those who suffer in this way are indestructible. Nothing can separate them from the love of God.

SUFFERING AND ATHEISM

Just when we come to accept that there is a suffering that makes us indestructible instead of destroying us, that teaches us to love life more than ever, that is when senseless suffering, in which all these possibilities are denied, becomes visible in all its horror. The letters of those who do not die for a cause, of children, of those who are caught up by chance, of innocent bystanders, testify to the horror of fruitless suffering. In their dying there is no pride, only lament. Their pain cannot be eliminated or given meaning. The suffering of one thrust unconsciously into the role of victim excludes every attempt to give meaning. The letter of a fourteen-year-old Jewish boy from Galilee, captured in a raid, contains this pain without hope of relief, without certainty or consolation.

My dear Parents,

If the heavens were paper and all people ink, I could not describe my grief and everything I see about me.

The camp is located in a clearing. From early morning on they compel us to work in the woods. My feet are bleeding, for someone took my shoes. We work the entire day with next to nothing to eat, and at night we sleep on the ground (someone took our coats as well).

Every night drunken soldiers come and beat us with blocks of wood, and the bruises make my body look like a charred piece of wood. Now and then someone tosses us a few carrots or a beet and

141

what happens is a scandal: people fighting to snatch a little piece or a leaf for themselves. The day before yesterday two boys escaped. Then they lined us up in a row and every fifth person was shot to death. I was not the fifth, but I know that I shall not get out of here alive. I say to all, farewell, dear Mama, dear Father, dear sisters and brothers, and I weep. . . . [22]

Over against such suffering every form of interpretation appears to be a type of optimism criticized by Schopenhauer, "not merely as an absurd, but also as a really *wicked* way of thinking, as a bitter mockery of the unspeakable suffering of humanity."[23] Even the attempt, taking Christ as the starting point, to give an interpretation of suffering as a way of learning which love must travel, is of little consequence in the face of imposed suffering. Christ's passion—understood as a process of learning to suffer, to live, and to die—can mean nothing for Chaim, the Jewish boy. Precisely for the sake of these people who suffer senselessly there would be need for an almighty and gracious God, but it is precisely the fate of these people that shatters any attempt to love such a God. In the face of senseless suffering the question arises: Where is this God? Is he watching? A young Communist girl writes her mother: "Your whole life has been a life of affliction. There is no God. When I was outside this place I often had my doubts about that, but now I know it for sure."[24]

The process that leads to the conclusion, "There is no God," can be seen almost as a normal development. Wherever people are confronted by senseless suffering, faith in a God who embodies both omnipotence and love has to waver or be destroyed. Under such circumstances this faith can be sustained only by a triumph of God's omnipotence, incompre-

22. Ibid., p. 254.
23. Arthur Schopenhauer, *The World as Will and Idea*, trans. R. B. Haldane and J. Kemp, Vol. 1 (London: Kegan Paul, Trench, Trübner and Co., Ltd., 1906⁵), p. 420 (Book 4, Chap. 59).
24. *Letzte Briefe* . . . , p. 284.

hensibility, somber joy over his love. Such a faith can **no** longer be oneness with the Father. It becomes mere submission to a stronger one.

The other answer to this God is more consistent—having no more to do with him. Brecht tells of a woman who has to sit and watch for many days as her grandmother's sister, a very pious woman, dies a tortured death. In her fever "she tried without ceasing to pray but, to her great distress, she had forgotten the words of the Lord's Prayer. This death shattered whatever faith in God I had left."[25] This is a common experience which few are spared. Its effect is a conscious atheism, the conviction that there is no gracious heavenly being still throned above destiny, controlling everything. Brecht does not tell this story as an isolated incident but as a terse depiction of what people experience along life's way in the modern world.

Atheism arises out of human suffering. A God who senselessly torments in death a woman who has dedicated her life to him cannot exist. To be sure, the faith that disintegrates in this experience is a theism that has almost nothing to do with Christ. Stories of this kind deal with God, never with Jesus. It is obvious that, as in the past, Christian proclamation and education hand on nothing else but the almighty Pharaoh. A questionnaire in various grades in school on what aspect of Christianity was most important brought references to God, to the immortality of the soul, and to moral, predominantly sexual, precepts. Christ didn't appear; no explanation was given of the name "Christian." Christ is unknown. The one who causes suffering and takes it away is proclaimed as God, not the one who suffers. As in the past God is the almighty ruler whose only relationship with suffering is that he causes or sends it and that he takes it away. Compared with faith in

25. Bertolt Brecht, "Karins Erzählungen," *Gesammelte Werke*, Vol. 11 (Frankfurt: Suhrkamp Verlag, 1967), p. 230.

this God, the growing atheism of the masses, despite its banality, is a step forward.

The banality of this atheism consists in the assumption that the questions that the great Pharaoh answered so unsatisfactorily are answered simply by deposing him. Merely to retreat from the problem of human suffering, merely to give up the question of theodicy is no solution. Nothing has happened when one considers suffering an insoluble issue and for that reason disregards it. Brecht disparaged even thinking about such suffering as "a bad habit" handed down from the time of metaphysical questions. "We must break ourselves of the habit of walking toward places that cannot be reached on foot . . . , thinking about problems that cannot be solved through thought."[26]

But the compulsion to break this habit appears to amount to repression. Love cannot resign itself to the senselessness of suffering and destruction. It cannot "break itself of the habit" of inquiring about people who are beyond help. The problems shoved aside by many Marxist thinkers—subjectivity, suffering, death—keep on cropping up again. It is impossible to retreat into a primitive state that predates these issues. The riches of subjectivity, as these have been unfolded, and their recognition depend according to Schopenhauer on the capacity to feel pain, which "reaches its highest degree in man. And then, again, the more distinctly a man knows, the more intelligent he is, the more pain he has. . . ."[27]

Indifference and the possibility of getting sidetracked dare not keep us from asking about the meaning of suffering, even if we don't succeed. Not retreat from the problem, but its conquest is necessary. Improper waiting for the one who causes and takes away suffering can be overcome, and people can answer the question about suffering with their own life,

26. Bertolt Brecht, "Meti," *Gesammelte Werke*, Vol. 12, p. 514.
27. Schopenhauer, op. cit., Vol. 1, p. 400 (Book 4, Chap. 56).

which has been "conformed to the image of Christ." It is not the stoic hero who with folded arms makes himself small, waits and keeps his distance in a state of indestructibility; it is not he who shows the possibility for humanizing suffering. Rather it is the mystic sufferer who opens his hands for everything coming his way. He has given up faith in and hope for a God who reaches into the world from outside, but not hope for changing suffering and learning from suffering.

THE CROSS

How can hope be expressed in the face of senseless suffering?

I begin with a story that Elie Wiesel, a survivor of Auschwitz, relates in his book *Night*:

The SS hung two Jewish men and a boy before the assembled inhabitants of the camp. The men died quickly but the death struggle of the boy lasted half an hour. "Where is God? Where is he?" a man behind me asked. As the boy, after a long time, was still in agony on the rope, I heard the man cry again, "Where is God now?" And I heard a voice within me answer, "Here he is —he is hanging here on this gallows. . . . "[28]

It is difficult to speak about this experience. One has not yet travelled the way that leads from the question to the answer simply by reflecting on it theologically. The reflection stands in danger of missing the way itself since it is bound to other situations and thus cannot comprehend the question.

Within Jewish religious thinking the answer given here is understood in terms of the shekinah, the "indwelling presence of God in the world." According to cabalistic teaching God does not forsake the suffering world, in need of redemption after the fall. "His glory itself descends to the world, enters into it, into 'exile,' dwells in it, dwells with the trou-

28. Elie Wiesel, *Night*, Foreword by François Mauriac, translated from the French by Stella Rodway (New York: Hill and Wang, 1960), pp. 70f.

bled, the suffering creatures in the midst of their uncleanness
—desiring to redeem them."[29] In his emptied, abased form
God shares the suffering of his people in exile, in prison, in
martyrdom. Wandering, straying, dispersed, his indwelling
rests in things and awaits the redemption of God through his
creatures. God suffers where people suffer. God must be delivered from pain. "It is not merely in appearance that God has
entered into exile in His indwelling in the world; it is not
merely in appearance that in His indwelling He suffers with
the fate of His world." So one can say that God, in the form
of this shekinah, hangs on the gallows at Auschwitz and waits
"for the initial movement toward redemption to come from
the world. . . . "[30] Redemption does not come to people from
outside or from above. God wants to use people in order to
work on the completion of his creation. Precisely for this reason God must also suffer with the creation.

To interpret this story within the framework of the Christian tradition, it is Christ who suffers and dies here. To be
sure, one must ask the effect of such an interpretation, which
connects Christ with those gassed in Auschwitz and those
burned with napalm in Vietnam. Wherever one compares the
incomparable—for instance, the Romans' judicial murder of
a first-century religious leader and the fascist genocide in the
twentieth century—there, in a sublime manner, the issue is
robbed of clarity, indeed the modern horror is justified. The
point of view from which the comparison proceeds is not the
number of victims nor the method of killing. A fifty-year-old
woman piece worker hangs on the cross no less than Jesus—
only longer. The only thing that can be compared is the
person's relationship to the suffering laid upon him, his learning, his change. The justification for a Christian interpreta-

29. Martin Buber, "Spinoza, Sabbatai Zvi, and the Baal-Shem," *The Origin and
Meaning of Hasidism,* ed. and trans. Maurice Friedman (New York: Horizon Press,
1960), p. 101.
30. Ibid., pp. 104f.

tion can only be established when it undergrids and clarifies what the story from Auschwitz contains.

In Jesus' passion history a decisive change occurs, the change from the prayer to be spared to the dreadfully clear awareness that that would not happen. The way from Gethsemane to Golgotha is a taking leave of (narcissistic) hope. It is the same change that occurs in the story from Auschwitz: the eye is directed away from the almighty Father to the sufferer himself. But not in such a way that this sufferer now has to endure everything alone. The essence of Jesus' passion history is the assertion that this one whom God forsook himself becomes God. Jesus does not die like a child who keeps waiting for his father. His "Eli, Eli" is a scream of growing up, the pain of this cry is a birth pang. When religion, which one can comprehend as the bundle of defense mechanisms against disappointment, intensifies one's holding fast to his father, then "faith [accomplishes] part of the task Freud assigns to whoever undertakes to 'do without his father'. . . ."[31]

The task of doing without one's father is accomplished in the story transmitted from Auschwitz, though to be sure in a way different from that in the mythical story of the death and resurrection of Christ. The mythical story is separated here, divided among individual voices. What Jesus experienced in himself is here assigned to three different characters. The man behind the narrator cries what Jesus cried; the boy died, as did Jesus; and the narrator hears a voice that tells him where God is, rather, *who* God is—the victim. But while Jesus is the question, victim, and answer in one person, in this story all communication breaks down. The questioner does not get the answer; the message does not reach the dying one, and the narrator remains alone with his voice, a fact one can scarcely endure.

31. Paul Ricoeur, *Freud and Philosophy: An Essay on Interpretation*, trans. Denis Savage (New Haven and London: Yale University Press, 1970), p. 548.

The decisive phrase, that God is hanging "here on this gallows," has two meanings. First, it is an assertion about God. God is no executioner—and no almighty spectator (which would amount to the same thing). God is not the mighty tyrant. Between the sufferer and the one who causes the suffering, between the victim and the executioner, God, whatever people make of this word, is on the side of the sufferer. God is on the side of the victim, he is hanged.

Second, it is an assertion about the boy. If it is not also an assertion about the boy, then the story is false and one can forget about the first assertion. But how can the assertion about the boy be made without cynicism? "He is with God, he has been raised, he is in heaven." Such traditional phrases are almost always clerical cynicism with a high apathy content. Sometimes one stammers such phrases which are in fact true as a child repeats something he doesn't understand, with confidence in the speaker and the language that has still not become part of him. That is always possible, but in the long run it destroys those who do it because learning to believe also means learning to speak, and it is theologically necessary to transcend the shells of our inherited language. What language can possibly serve not only to preserve for all the life asserted by classical theology but primarily to translate it into a language of liberation? We would have to learn to hear the confession of the Roman centurian, "Truly this was God's son," in the phrase, "Here he is—he is hanging here on this gallows." Every single one of the six million was God's beloved son. Were anything else the case, resurrection would not have occurred, even in Jesus' case.

God is not in heaven; he is hanging on the cross. Love is not an otherworldly, intruding, self-asserting power—and to meditate on the cross can mean to take leave of that dream.

Precisely those who in suffering experience the strength of

the weak, who incorporate the suffering into their lives, for whom coming through free of suffering is no longer the highest goal, precisely they are there for the others who, with no choice in the matter, are crucified in lives of senseless suffering. A different salvation, as the language of metaphysics could promise it, is no longer possible. The God who causes suffering is not to be justified even by lifting the suffering later. No heaven can rectify Auschwitz. But the God who is not a greater Pharaoh has justified himself: in sharing the suffering, in sharing the death on the cross.

God has no other hands than ours. Even "the future," which today is often supposed to translate the mythical word "heaven," cannot alter the fact that the boy had to die that way in Auschwitz, that in our century children like Chaim had to write such letters. But perhaps this future can preserve the memory of these children and thereby put up a better fight against death.

It is no less significant for us than it is for the boy that God is the one hanging on this gallows. God has no other hands than ours, which are able to act on behalf of other children.

The objection can be raised that even with this thought the dead are still "being used" for the living. They are to help us, to change us. That is perhaps true—but is any other relationship with the dead conceivable? Doesn't all remembering of them and all praying for them, all eating in remembrance of them have this character, that we "need" the dead in a double sense, of wanting them and of making use of them? They have been taken from us and are unable to prevent this use of themselves. But there is no way for us to love them other than to incorporate them into our work at living. There is no other way but to consume them—and perhaps that represents a debt we owed them that cannot be paid in life. Through our behavior we can turn them into "the devil's martyrs" posthumously, who confirm the eternal cycle of injustice under the sun and bring ourselves to speechlessness; or we can use them for praise to God.

In this sense those who suffer in vain and without respect depend on those who suffer in accord with justice. If there were no one who said, "I die, but I shall live," no one who said, "I and the Father are one," then there would be no hope for those who suffer mute and devoid of hoping. All suffering would then be senseless, destructive pain that could not be worked on, all grief would be "worldly grief" and would lead to death. But we know of people who have lived differently, suffered differently. There is a history of resurrections, which has vicarious significance. A person's resurrection is no personal privilege for himself alone—even if he is called Jesus of Nazareth. It contains within itself hope for all, for everything.

6

The Religion of Slaves

Basically, the secret of life is to act as though we possessed the thing we most painfully lack. In that lies the whole doctrine of Christianity. To convince ourselves that everything *is* created for good, that the brotherhood of man *really exists* —and if that is not true, what does it matter? The comfort of this vision lies in believing it, not in whether it is real. For if I believe it, and you, and he, and everyone, it will become real.[1]

SIMONE WEIL, TOUJOURS ANTIGONE

We can approach the theme of suffering by starting with situations involving suffering and showing how they were understood and what changes they evoked. But it is at least equally important to set before us people who have suffered consciously, people we know who in suffering have become better and not more bitter, those who have willingly taken suffering upon themselves for the sake of others. There are such

1. Cesare Pavese, *This Business of Living. Diary: 1935–50*, ed. and trans. A. E. Murch (London: Peter Owen Ltd., 1961), p. 151 (February 3, 1941). Copyright © 1961 by Peter Owen Ltd. Reprinted by permission.

people, and the strength that goes forth from them is the consolation of the saints.

Perhaps one day people will number among this century's saints the French Jewess Simone Weil, although she was more ready "to die for the church than to join it." She never allowed the slightest distinction between thinking and acting. Her philosophical and theological thinking, teaching, and writing were in accord with her activity in the workers' movement and later in the resistance against Hitler. She was at home at the borders and contact points of varied realms: mathematics and mysticism, Judaism and Catholicism, ancient philosophy and Marxism, these are among the varied realms in her thought. The borders, or as she herself says, the "threshhold" (that is, neither the house nor the street), appears to be her preferred dwelling place, the only one that suits her. She was a Christian in a non-confessional sense, who did not, however, submit to baptism. For then she would have betrayed her truth, precisely that at the threshhold, "if I had left the point, where I have been since my birth, at the intersection of Christianity and everything that is not Christianity. I have always remained at this exact point, on the threshhold of the Church, without moving, quite still, *en hupomenē* (in patience). . . . "[2]

Simone Weil came from a well-to-do Jewish family. She grew up in Paris, went to college, and became a teacher until one day she applied for a one year leave of absence in order to work as an unskilled worker in an electrical factory, later as a milling machine operator for Renault. She took an assumed name, rented a room near the factory, and tried to arrange her life in such a way that it was no different from that of her co-workers. Unaccustomed to such physical exertion, she found

2. Simone Weil, "Letter Four, Spiritual Autobiography," *Waiting For God*, trans. Emma Craufurd, with an introduction by Leslie A. Fiedler (New York: G. P. Putnam's Sons, 1951), p. 76. Copyright © 1951 by G. P. Putnam's Sons. Reprinted by permission.

it an agony, since from childhood on she suffered severe headaches almost constantly. She reflected on these experiences in a report on *La Condition ouvrière* (working cond`i`tions) which, like almost everything she wrote, appeared only after her death. One part of this work was the "Journal d'usine," a diary about this experiment carried out under the most difficult conditions imaginable. On December 17, 1934, for example, she wrote:

Tired and discouraged, on account of a weak constitution; a sensation of having been a free person for 24 hours (on Sunday) and now again having to accustom myself to a slave-existence. . . . Against your will, for the sake of these 56 centimes (the price per piece in piece work), the necessity to exert yourself and spend yourself with the certain prospect of a reprimand for slowness or for ruining something . . . a feeling of slavery.[3]

As a middle class intellectual, a graduate of the École Normale Supèrieure where they gave her the nickname "Vierge rouge" (the Red Virgin), she attempted to try out the conditions of proletarian existence on her own body, weakened through sickness and overexertion. Already as a young teacher out in the country she had become an advocate of the workers and the unemployed, worked in the union and taken part in marches and demonstrations, so that she was summoned, warned, and finally transferred by the school authorities.

After Hitler's occupation of France in 1940 Simone Weil lived with her parents in temporarily unoccupied Southern France. During that period she became absorbed in Greek and philosophy, learned Sanskrit, occupied herself with mysticism, and at the same time worked in the resistance. In the spring of 1942, after resisting the idea for a long while, she

3. Simone Weil, *La Condition ouvrière* (Paris, 1951), cited from Angelica Krogmann, *Simone Weil* (Hamburg: Rowohlt, 1970), p. 67.

was ready to emigrate to the United States with her parents. But she stood it only a short time, although mysticism and Sanskrit of course would have been available there also. She travelled to England, where she was active under Maurice Schumann in the service of the French regime in exile. Here too her place was on the border between contempletive mysticism and political action.

Since as a Jewess she could not take part actively in the struggle for France, she went the way of solidarity through sharing the suffering. She restricted herself to the same rations to which the French were entitled by their food cards, rations which in France itself could be exceeded in many cases. Thus, put on a level with the poorest and most helpless, her suffering grew so much worse that she had to enter the hospital in the spring of 1943. She died on August 24, 1943 in a sanatorium in Ashford, Kent, at the age of 34.

Simone Weil's theme is suffering. Through Antigone's fate she made clear again and again what awaits those who contradict the standard that prevails everywhere, the division into friends and enemies. Creon says to Antigone, "A foe is never a friend—not even in death," and Antigone answers him with the famous words, " 'Tis not my nature to join in hating, but in loving."[4]

Sophocles is not interested here in a general ideology about humanity, and, correspondingly, Simone Weil also turns attention away from the common confession, and the appeal not to join in hating but in suffering, and refers to the fate of love in the world. Creon's answer to the famous words of Antigone are clear and horrible, for they show that those who participate only in love and not in hate belong to another world and have to expect a violent death. Creon says, "Pass, then, to the

---

4. Sophocles, "Antigone," trans. R. C. Jebb, *The Complete Greek Drama*, ed. W. J. Oates and Eugene O'Neill, Jr., Vol. 1 (New York: Random House, 1938), p. 436 (lines 522 f.).

world of the dead, and, if thou must needs love, love them."[5] Sophocles would be just as misunderstood as Christ if one separated his call for love from his and love's fate, from the cross.

The Christian faith relates to suffering not merely as remover or consoler. It offers no "supernatural remedy for suffering" but strives for "a supernatural use for it."[6] A person's wounds are not taken from him. Even the risen Christ still had his scars. But what does it mean not to remove suffering but to "use" it differently?

Suffering makes people cry out "why"? That question sounds, as Simone Weil says, through the entire Iliad; it is Christ's cry as well. If it could be answered, it would be possible to explain and offer consolation for suffering. But Christianity dispels this illusion.

There is no reply. When one finds a comforting reply, first of all one has constructed it oneself. . . . If the word "why" expressed the search for a cause, the reply would appear easily. But it expresses the search for an end. This whole universe is empty of finality. The soul which, because it is torn by affliction, cries out continually for this finality, touches the void.[7]

Simone Weil has defined this void, the absence of God, as a horror that submerges the entire soul. "During this absence there is nothing to love."[8] This definition of affliction pinpoints its "inconsolable bitterness." We are destroyed most thoroughly by that affliction that robs us of any possibility of loving any longer. The temptation to commit suicide, a temptation into which every normal person falls according to

5. Ibid., p. 437 (lines 524f).
6. Simone Weil, *Gravity and Grace,* with an Introduction by Gustave Thibon, trans. Arthur Wills (New York: G. P. Putnam's Sons, 1952), p. 132. Copyright © 1952 by G. P. Putnam's Sons. Reprinted by permission.
7. Simone Weil, *Intimations of Christianity Among the Ancient Greeks,* collected and translated from the French by Elisabeth Chase Geissbuhler (Boston: Beacon Press, 1957), pp. 198f.
8. Simone Weil, "The Love of God and Affliction," *Waiting for God,* p. 121.

Camus, makes precisely this offer—since we are no longer able to love, it offers to remove also the desire to love and to make us once and for all free of all relationships. The affliction, fear, depression, destruction, which the loss of the person on whom we had built our life represents—all of that threatens the capacity we need the most, the capacity to keep on loving. "What is terrible is that if, in this darkness where there is nothing to love, the soul ceases to love, God's absence becomes final."[9] This is precisely what death is, separation from everything life can actually signify.

The only salvation for a person in this despair is to go on loving "in the void," a love for God that is no longer reactive, in answer to experienced happiness—the gratitude of a child —but instead an act that goes beyond all that has been experienced. "The soul has to go on loving in the emptiness, or at least to go on wanting to love, though it may only be with an infinitesimal part of itself. Then, one day, God will come to show himself to this soul. . . . "[10]

If it does not renounce loving, it happens one day to hear, not a reply to the question which it cries, for there is none, but the very silence as something infinitely more full of significance than any response, like God himself speaking. It knows then that God's absence here below is the same thing as the secret presence upon earth of the God who is in heaven.[11]

One must not be confused by the words used here, like "God" or "soul," or by their relation to one another, as if the experience described here were accessible only to those who had a clear understanding of these concepts. I do not presuppose here answers to questions about what the soul is or how much it needs God in order to live. These are not presupposi-

9. Ibid.
10. Ibid.
11. Simone Weil, *Intimations of Chrisianity*, p. 199.

tions for the process but its result. This process itself contains two elements that are essential to a faith that is not inherited or merely "fabricated."

The first is the dark night of despair, the cross, on which we are hammered without being asked. A Christian is a person whose death is behind him. "You were dead," is a recurring expression in the Bible. It is the death of being without any relationships, the "I can't any longer," the scream. Suffering causes death, and no one gets around this death. The child we once were dies. The youth with his inexhaustible vitality also dies. Our dreams and illusions die.

We don't have the choice of avoiding suffering and going around all these deaths. The only choice we have is between the absurd cross of meaninglessness and the cross of Christ, the death we accept apathetically as a natural end and the death we suffer as a passion.

The second element is resurrection. If in the night of despair the soul does not cease loving "in the void," then the object of its love can rightly be called "God." We can also speak of an unending affirmation of life that arises in the dark night of the cross. This formulation avoids the appearance that it is necessary to have a personal relationship to a God thought of as a person. The mystical experience of the night of the cross and of the light within it is not dependent on such a personally interpreted relationship to God. Analogously Simone Weil also regards the concept of personal immortality more as a hindrance than an aid to faith. Decisive for resurrection is the question whether the person in the death of the natural man, in the destruction of the immediacy of life, can keep on loving.

The capacity not to stop loving depends on faith in God, if we understand thereby that the totality of the world is not meaningless, empty, capricious, and indifferent to man, but instead for him. But how can a person whose whole family was tortured to death and who had himself been tortured for a long time in a concentration camp believe in this compassion of God? "Such men if they had previously believed in the mercy of God would either believe in it no longer, or else they would conceive of it quite differently than before."[12] Faith in this compassion cannot be derived directly from nature or grounded in it. Every attempt of this kind presupposes that we blind our eyes, stop our ears, and tear out all compassion. This kind of "faith," in meaning that is demonstrable in the course of history, in compassion and justice to which one can point, leads the faithful only to an absence of compassion. Paradox remains a necessary form for the Christian faith, not insight derived from nature and history. *Credo, non video* (I believe, though I do not see): I see the injustice, the destruction, the senseless suffering—I believe the justice, the coming liberation, the love that occurs in the night of the cross. But precisely this unfounded faith in compassion is the religion of slaves.

BLESSED ARE THOSE WHO SUFFER

After my year in the factory, before going back to teaching, I had been taken by my parents to Portugal, and while there I left them to go alone to a little village. I was, as it were, in pieces, soul and body. That contact with affliction had killed my youth. Until then I had not had any experience of affliction, unless we count my own, which, as it was my own, seemed to me, to have little importance, and which moreover was only a partial affliction, being biological and not social.

I knew quite well that there was a great deal of affliction in the world, I was obsessed with the idea, but I had not had prolonged and first-hand experience of it. As I worked in the factory, indistinguishable to all eyes, including my own, from the anonymous mass, the affliction of others entered into my flesh and my soul. Nothing separated me from it, for I had really forgotten my past

12. Simone Weil, *Gravity and Grace*, p. 168.

and I looked forward to no future, finding it difficult to imagine the possibility of surviving all the fatigue. What I went through there marked me in so lasting a manner that still today when any human being, whoever he may be and in whatever circumstances, speaks to me without brutality, I cannot help having the impression that there must be a mistake and that unfortunately the mistake will in all probability disappear. There I received forever the mark of a slave, like the branding of the red-hot iron the Romans put on the foreheads of their most despised slaves. Since then I have always regarded myself as a slave.

In this state of mind then, and in a wretched condition physically, I entered the little Portugese village, which, alas, was very wretched too, on the very day of the festival of its patron saint. I was alone. It was the evening and there was a full moon over the sea. The wives of the fishermen were, in procession, making a tour of all the ships, carrying candles and singing what must certainly be very ancient hymns of a heart-rending sadness. Nothing can give any idea of it. I have never heard anything so poignant unless it were the song of the boatmen on the Volga. There the conviction was suddenly borne in upon me that Christianity is pre-eminently the religion of slaves, that slaves cannot help belonging to it, and I among others.[13]

Christianity exists for slaves. It is the religion of the oppressed, of those marked by affliction. It concerns itself with their needs. People are pronounced blessed not because of their achievments or their behavior, but with regard to their needs. Blessed are the poor, the suffering, the persecuted, the hungry.

The text above is also nothing else but a beatitude. It comes from a letter of Simone Weil's, written about May 15, 1942, prior to her emigration for America. The letter speaks about suffering, but above all it expresses a boundless affirmation of life, even the life of a slave. Those who are amazed when they are addressed without brutality, when they are not used and treated as commodities—the religion of slaves exists

13. Simone Weil, Letter from about May 15, 1942, *Waiting For God*, pp. 66f.

precisely for them. Not that they should remain slaves thereby, but that they should thereby stand, arise. I am not referring to the religion of slavery which perpetuates slavery, but rather to the religion of those unfortunate for a time to whom life is promised. Their suffering, their rights, their truth are expressed.

"Christianity has sided with all that is weak and base, with all failures; it has made an ideal of whatever *contradicts* the instinct of the strong life to preserve itself. . . . "[14] This siding with the less fit, less valuable or strong has been seen by no one more clearly than by one of Christianity's harshest critics, Friedrich Nietzsche. Christianity arose among "the lowest classes, the *underworld* of the ancient world,"[15] and through this religion "everything miserable that suffers from itself, that is afflicted with bad feelings, the whole ghetto-world of the soul [is] *on top* all at once."[16] It was precisely all the failures, all the rebellious-minded, all the less favored, the whole scum and refuse of humanity who were ". . . won over to it."[17] Christianity is a rebellion of everything that crawls on the ground against that which has *height*: "the evangel of the 'lowly' *makes* low."[18]

This religion of slaves is not only a religious-spiritual assigning of value, but it is at the same time a political movement of rebellion. "All who were secretly rebellious, the whole inheritance of anarchistic agitation in the Empire"[19] rumbled within it. The historical recognition of Christianity's proletarian origins, used by Kautsky in a socialistic sense, is seen also by Nietzsche, who considers this religion to be the result of a class conflict provoked by the powerless in search of

14. Friedrich Nietzsche, "The Antichrist," *The Portable Nietzsche*, selected and translated, with an introduction, prefaces, and notes by Walter Kaufmann (New York: Viking Press, 1968), p. 571.
15. Ibid., p. 589.
16. Ibid., p. 651.
17. Ibid., p. 619.
18. Ibid., p. 620.
19. Ibid., p. 649.

power. Thus Nietzsche attacks socialists and Christians simultaneously. Both demand equal rights for all people, both fight for the slaves. "The 'equality of souls before God,' this falsehood, this *pretext* for the rancor of all the baseminded, this explosive of a concept which eventually became revolution, modern idea, and the principle of decline of the whole order of society—is *Christian* dynamite."[20] Correspondingly, Jesus is also classified in political terms and regarded as a criminal —something that clearly contracts several other statements of Nietzsche's about Jesus. "That holy anarchist who summoned the people at the bottom, the outcasts and 'sinners,' . . . to opposition against the dominant order—using language, if the Gospels were to be trusted, which would lead to Siberia today too—was a political criminal. . . . This brought him to the cross. . . ."[21]

Christianity is the morality of slaves who deny and destroy the values of their masters. At its center stands a value which evokes Nietzsche's harshest criticism: pity. "Pity is the *practice* of nihilism."[22] It produces more and more weakness. It is hostile to life and multiplies misery. As an expression of decadence it favors those whose suffering corresponds to reality —which means for Nietzsche a reality of failure. "Quite in general, pity crosses the law of development, which is the law of *selection*. It preserves what is ripe for destruction; it defends those who have been disinherited and condemned by life. . . ."[23] One can only agree with Nietzsche's presentation of what Christianity seeks. It is in fact the religion of those who have been disinherited and condemned by life. Contrary to all vitalism and all worship of the healthy and strong, Christianity sees life better preserved by those who have already died once. God "will not break a bruised reed, or snuff out a

20. Ibid., p. 655.
21. Ibid., p. 197.
22. Ibid., p. 573.
23. Ibid.

smouldering wick" (Isa. 42:3, NEB)—contrary to all principles of selection. From a Christian point of view life is loved more deeply and comprehensively where even the weak and the maimed share, both as givers and receivers, in this love for life. Faith, with its non-selective affirmation, opposes natural as well as historical selection.

Nietzsche correctly sees that the " 'instinctive exclusion of any antipathy, any hostility, any boundaries or divisions in man's feelings' [is] the consequence of an extreme capacity for suffering and excitement . . . which finds blessedness (pleasure) only in no longer offering any resistance to anybody, neither to evil nor to him who is evil. . . . "[24] The affirmation which Christianity asserts and formulates as its faith actually develops a deeper capacity for suffering because the aspiration on behalf of all and the pain with all has become boundless. "Boundaries and divisions" have always been the concern of the upper classes; elite privileges were secured thereby. The abolition of all privileges is the primary presupposition for a concept of love that can be socially relevant beyond I-Thou relationships and which has been relevant in groups again and again. Nietzsche's vitalism proceeds selectively. Christian faith is comprehensive, unbounded affirmation. The "exclusion of any antipathy, any hostility" is not, with Nietzsche, to be construed as weakness which contradicts the instinct for self-preservation, but as strength which leads to the change-producing acceptance of suffering. But again, how is such a non-selective affirmation possible unless we practice "God's reconciliation with misery?"

THE PARADOX

The symbol for the religion of slaves is the cross, the kind of punitive death reserved for slaves. Is it necessary for this symbol of suffering, of failure, of dying, to stand at the mid-

24. Ibid., p. 602.

point of the Christian religion? Has not an overemphasis on the cross in theology and piety resulted in the fact that a "God who justifies misery" was and is worshipped in society? Ulrich Hedinger has attacked the "alliance between antiquity and Christianity" because of their fundamental doctrine that "a supreme Providence rules over or by harsh fate," and radically rejected any commendation of submission. The cross cannot be made the center of a messianically understood theology that abolishes misery. Jesus' death was first and foremost a religio-political and political assassination, and love, "even Jesus' forgiving love, does not require assassination by crucifixion in order to be authentic."[25] In this context Hedinger criticizes theological thinking that elevates the paradox, the unresolved contradiction to suffering-filled reality, to the central theological category. "Where God is the paradox in an absolute sense, there he clouds the distinction between love and misery."[26]

But the question whether love requires the cross in order to be authentic appears to me to be posed falsely. In the context of this question Hedinger understands the cross either as a "metaphysic of punitive death," that is, from the perspective of the God who ordains suffering, who finally has a chance to complete Abraham's sacrifice, or he takes it as a "mysticism of consolation for death," which people receive for their own suffering and dying in view of the cross. But the cross is neither a symbol expressing the relationship between God the Father and his Son nor a symbol of masochism which needs suffering in order to convince itself of love. It is above all a symbol of reality. Love does not "require" the cross, but *de facto* it ends up on the cross. *De facto* Jesus of Nazareth was crucified; *de facto* the crosses of the rebellious slaves under

---

25. Ulrich Hedinger, *Wider die Versöhnung Gottes mit dem Elend. Eine Kritik des christlichen Theismus und Atheismus* (Zürich: Theologischer Verlag, 1972), p. 154.
26. Ibid., p. 149.

Spartacus adorned the streets of the Roman empire. The cross is no theological invention but the world's answer, given a thousand times over, to attempts at liberation. Only for that reason are we able to recognize ourselves in Jesus' dying on the cross. We observe the ideology of the rulers who supported the prevailing order. We see the brutality and sadism of the soldiers, who had a hand in it, following orders. We are confronted by the behavior of friends. All these are possibilities for our behavior toward the stricken. And when we ourselves are struck by affliction, then we can try to learn from the story of Jesus. The question whether love needs the cross for its actualization holds only a speculative and not an existential interest. Nor does God's *doxa*, his splendor, his self-revealing glory, his happiness, "need" the dreadful paradoxes of the destruction and mutilation of life if one considers God in that light. But *de facto* love ends up on the cross and within visible reality God chooses to act paradoxically.

Love does not cause suffering or produce it, though it must necessarily seek confrontation, since its most important concern is not the avoidance of suffering but the liberation of people. Jesus' suffering was avoidable. He endured it voluntarily. There were other ways out, as is stressed again and again in mythical language: it would have been possible for him to come down from the cross and allow himself to be helped. To put it in political terms, he didn't need to go to Jerusalem and could have avoided the confrontation. To avoid confrontation by giving up certain goals is one of the most common forms of apathetic behavior; to seek confrontation is a form of behavior necessary for those who suffer and aspire. This can be demonstrated through many experiences in the civil rights movements of recent years. The officials in charge usually practice a policy of appeasement, delay, and cover-up. The citizens who are taking part, on the other hand, seek and produce confrontation as they make suffering visible.

Their suffering would be avoidable only under conditions they neither can nor want to fulfill. To reconcile God with misery means precisely avoiding confrontation and, in fear of being formed in the image of Christ, which includes pain, putting off liberating love.

This applies also to all individual relationships. If it is true that a person's riches consist in the riches of his human relationships then the pain that grows out of these relationships belongs necessarily to our riches. The more we love, the more people in whom we take an interest, the more closely we are bound to them, the more likely it is that we get into difficulties and experience pain. The failure of love, its experienced futility, points people to a sense of assurance, a consolation that is expressed theologically with the model of the paradox. The hope for a better future must be firmly established in the present, as consolation for the people who are now suffering. God must also be thought of as present with those who are in misery, and thereby the truth even of love that has not yet achieved its goal remains certain.

If God is not already intervening directly to help, to rescue, to manifest himself as salvation, then the consolation of the future, without any present, is an abstraction. When Hedinger asks us to choose "future or paradox" he is posing false alternatives. There is no future if the people who can experience it merely wait for a later time as they suffer without actually experiencing its truth, its meaning. The paradox—that God loves us even when nothing of that is visible—is, from a subjective perspective, what makes the future possible. If there were no paradox, then the future would not be for all but only for those who were still around to experience it.

With this paradox Christianity has created for itself a thought-form that stresses the strength of those who now believe and not the future strength of God, who brings in his kingdom.

Yea, whate'er I here must bear,
Thou art still my purest Pleasure,
Jesus, priceless Treasure![27]

That is not merely depth of passion—to say nothing of resignation. It is mystical defiance. The paradox is a snare in which we catch God. He cannot cut us down to size. As he acts punitively or experiments with us—which we also experience as destruction—we, against experience, hold to the contraction of love. The meaning of the cross is not to reconcile God with misery and finish us off in the paradox. The unity of cross and resurrection, failure and victory, weeping and laughing, makes the utopia of a better life possible for the first time. He who does not weep needs no utopia; to him who only weeps God remains mute.

The Christian God is no little Chinese god of fortune, as Brecht extols him, in whose kingdom it is possible to remain free of want and sorrow. Jesus—multiplying loaves and healing the sick—could have had all this; indeed can have it. Instead Jesus identified with the suffering and for the sake of their sicknesses became sick; for the sufferers' sake he suffered abuse; in order to overcome death he, like everyone else, became mortal. To accept the way of Jesus means also to hold on to the paradox.

Of course one needs to see that the paradox is a category that in the strict sense applies to the individual. The justification of misery in society through a theology of paradox is a macabre perspective. If the rich, white nations recommend to the hungry paradox and not liberation, then paradox becomes a theological-imperialistic trick. But even understood individually one can perhaps demonstrate and show this "joy in sorrow" but hardly recommend it verbally or use it in pastoral care. A person can perhaps suffer for another, but he

27. Johann Franck, "Jesus, Priceless Treasure" (Translation composite), 1653.

cannot accomplish the acceptance of pain for the other person. He can help him by mourning with him, but he cannot fulfill for him the task of "serving the pain of God with your own pain." He cannot make suffering productive for another. That remains the task for the mature individual himself. We can only help one another with suggestions—and if this book tries to get people to use their pain productively and to love their life even if it is full of sorrow, then the paradox is understood as an aid in the process of liberation.

An objection arises again and again to this tendency of encouragement toward a humanizing suffering. Aren't such considerations written only for the strong? Don't they presuppose a measure of maturity, ego-strength, power, will-to-live, which is precisely what sufferers lack most of all? Isn't the capacity for acceptance tied to childhood conditions of extreme happiness, experiences of approval, as we found them, for example, in the life story of Jacques Lusseyran? What about the many others? Will they not put aside this attempt to learn from suffering, as all other such attempts, because it is precisely their affliction which appears to leave open for them no chance of this kind, no possibility for change? I'm thinking of many young people who regard themselves as "worthless." The political frustration they have experienced in various realms of life has increased their irritability but not their capacity to suffer. It has strengthened their great fear of growing up. They see with extreme clarity the difficulty of assuming responsibility in a system that sets up barriers to any real assumption of responsibility and turns to its own advantage the meager benefits and responsibilities it offers. Suffering at the hands of society and the psychological difficulties of individuals become a vicious circle in which healing is regarded almost as mere conformity and the mentally ill as the only ones who are acting normally. The number of those who dare to understand suffering at society's hands, as well as their own suffering, as a productive force is too small; the attempt to avoid suffering too great.

Many attach themselves to political groups in part because they sense a need for security, love, and freedom from fear. But they are also often disappointed with their own groups, because competitive and power-oriented thinking prevails in the inner sanctum of the ideologically likeminded and the weak surrender to those who can speak better and possess "an almost absolute psychological power-monoply. The psychological misery continues to exist,"[28] and has to continue to exist, as long as the entire force of such groups is directed toward criticism, destruction, and fighting and the possibilities for affirmation prohibited and made intellectually reprehensible. But that for which the fight is being waged must remain capable of expression; we have to be able to anticipate it—in celebration, in play. The language of analysis and exhortation alone does not suffice. It is necessary to find a native language in which desires can be put into words.

The possibilities for open-ended affirmation, for emotional self-expression, and for self-realization, a place free of fear, in which people can communicate with one another, these depend on a deeper love for life, which needs to be expressed in words, dance, and song. If God may nowhere be praised anymore, if the view prevails that in this phony life there is nothing true and nothing worthy of praise, then the fears multiply one upon another. Political groups of the left bring together people who affirm life comprehensively and for everyone. Unfortunately this is obscured and obstructed for the members of the group through a mind-set continually bent on destruction. One's own weakness must then at all costs be kept hidden. Suffering remains destructive, those oppressed by it see no sense in this present life and frequently seize at middle-

28. "Angstüberwindung und Selbstbefreiung," a Mannheim paper of the SDS, 1969.

class conformity as the only possibility of ending suffering. Thus they transform, after the fact, what was more than a youth movement into precisely that. They then fall prey to middle-class apathy in a worse way than their fathers, because they know what they are doing and they have to keep on working at the suppression of this consciousness. Without the paradox that even in this phony life the other life can appear and blossom, hope becomes hopeless. Without unceasing affirmation the radically critical attitude turns against the one negating everything and delivers him helplessly to a suffering devoid of learning.

Thereby a perception of how one's own pain can "serve the pain of God in the world" would be gained most quickly by this generation, whose sensibility contains so much more reality, perception of the suffering of others, so much less pure *weltschmerz* than that of comparable youth movements.

> We can heed the call,
> We can trip and fall.
> We can read the scrawl on the garden wall.
> Let the ashes fall upon us all,
> Or none at all—it's in us all.
>
> Can we say it's cool
> From a heated pool
> When we give a jewel to a starving fool?
> And if we can't be cruel, then let us take the tool
> And change the rule, and change the rule.
>
> When we've all begun
> To see the world we're on.
> Don't you see there's only one?
> Then we all begin to see the skin we're in.
> It's just the same—there's only one.
>
> Do we have the grace
> To begin the race

In another place, face to face?
Do we stand the pace or do we let the case
Go to waste, go to waste, go to waste?[29]

This song's final question is a question about humanizing suffering. Can it become productive—or must we let ashes fall on us? At the very least we can increase the number of people who experience their own suffering without fear and are strengthened by it. It is natural for us to turn from suffering, to seek wherever possible to escape it, to minimize and suppress it in ourselves and in others. It is natural to close our eyes when we see someone suffering. Because of this natural brutality people die. Can this brutality be humanized?

Humanity's past experiences contract hope; but not completely, not hopelessly. There are ways out by means of a different kind of compassion, even if these ways are narrow and virtually hidden through pain. They do not consist in flight or prevention but in a more comprehensive acceptance of reality, loving life so much that our affirmation includes the injury and the pain! We can avoid much suffering and the bitterness of suffering, but only for a price that is too high—ceasing to love. Then it doesn't hurt us; then we don't end up on the cross; then we belong to those with unblemished skin and an ongoing share in the good life.

> Can we say it's cool
> From a heated pool . . . ?

But then we forsake others and ourselves; we have sold our souls. Then we affirm only a little slice of reality, not the whole of reality in whose midst stands the cross.

---

29. Record "There's Only One" on Graham Nash, "Songs for Beginners" (Atlantic 50006). Copyright © 1971 Giving Room Music, Inc. Used by permission. All rights reserved.

"THERE IS NO ALIEN SORROW"

Nevertheless there remains the question about those who suffer senselessly and are destroyed. It can only be attacked—not finally answered—by those who learn in suffering. They will not give up the attempt at change. Nor will they stop at the boundaries of this attempt. Where *nothing* can be done, they will join in the suffering.

Aside from a sentimental shudder, compassion is not natural or self-evident. The instinct of hens to fall upon the wounded is softened only slightly among us. In a film about Vietnam the Russian poet Konstantin Simonov comments on the pictures of the destruction of houses.

In order to understand other people's affliction, apparently one must, at least once in his lifetime, at least for a minute, put himself in their shoes.

Let's try to imagine the fate of this family, or this one, or that one over there, if they didn't live in Texas or Rhode Island but in the province of Nang Na or Quang Binh. You, together with your whole family, O.K.? That is your husband. And do you know that they shot him to death from the helicopter as he came through the jungle? And your eldest son was smashed to pieces by a plastic mine that was dropped from an American plane. And your middle son was killed in an air raid. And a shell fragment from an American cruiser hit the younger son. And this one, the smallest, remained alive at first. They poured a little napalm over him; they tried afterwards to save him in the hospital, but they couldn't. And you are alone. It does't take long to kill only five people.

No, that didn't happen to you. I'm giving you back your family. You are together again, thank God.

But this woman, she really has no one. She remains alone, alone. So try to imagine that it all didn't happen to her but to you, and not sometime in the remote past, but yesterday, today, now. I have given them back to you. I took them from you only to get you to think about it, at least for a minute, and gave them back again. And her? One can give her no one back. She is alone.

Under the bombs,
to save them from death,
one snatches, for the hundredth night,
the children from their beds.
Under the bombs
they must hide in the daytime,
and in the night
someone wakes them up.
He is five, he nine already.
Against them weapons are arrayed.
What the children want most of all
is three months' sleep.
They hear the bombs
that strike father and mother.
Nevertheless
they want to sleep.
No conscience wakes them any longer
at the right time.
Nothing any longer takes the sleeplessness
from these eyes.
And the doctors have no pills
to rescue from these nights
these children's childhood.[30]

"There is no sorrow that is alien sorrow," says Simonov. That is not a sentence stating observable facts. It is a wish, a hope that lives on the presupposed brotherhood of all mankind. It cannot be proven why there is no alien sorrow, no distant sorrow that does not concern us. Every proof for such a sentence makes it poorer and smaller. It is not deducible. It is much rather something one lays on the conscience of a thinking and feeling being. Wherever there is suffering, that is a concern of yours. That those who suffer belong together, not to be separated from the others, that pain cannot be parcelled out into friends and enemies, that is part of the religion of slaves. There is no alien sorrow, we are all a part of it, we

30. Konstantin Simonov, "There is No Alien Sorrow," film commentary.

share in it. They will say of our time that it was the time of the war in Vietnam. And we shall be asked where we stood, whether we shared the suffering or aided those who caused it. Suffering tolerates no neutrality, no Pilate-standpoint.

In mythological language it was possible to say that God will wipe away all tears. It is a language that seeks justice on behalf of those defrauded of their lives. It is the language of a love which will not let itself be consoled prematurely. This language of myth was interpreted in the context of a metaphysical worldview that spoke of two places and times. If this interpretation has become impossible, that is, if it means nothing any longer and its consolation—of a continuing life and of a reunion in heaven—can console no one any longer, then the question remains whether there is another interpretation of that which was promised in mythological language. The sentence, "There is no alien sorrow," points in the direction of such an alternative interpretation of what formerly could be stated only by reference to the two worlds.

That God will wipe away tears can no longer be accepted in a direct sense. The fourteen-year-old Jewish boy Chaim is dead. From what face will God wipe away the tears? The God conceived of in that way comes too late. But if God is not thought of as an alien superior power but as that which occurs between people, then the relationship to this child does not end with death. Then it is not over and done with in the course of an individual life. There is too much left unfulfilled in this life. There is no alien sorrow: this sentence includes even the dead. Their pain is ours, their death is not simply the "death of others," radically different from mine. We can live in such a way that our life portrays a hope that other children will suffer no longer.

One can object: what good does that do for Chaim and the other dead children? But this objection grows out of a limited perspective that sees existence in terms of individual lives. But this is a limited perspective our thought and experience will surpass. If there will no longer be any alien sorrow, then there is also no alien life. Then the destruction or rescue of a life always means destruction or rescue for all. Then the hope for Chaim, that our children no longer have to suffer, is a hope that one cannot hold off by asking what help it is to him. A person actually has a share in the life that is no longer his but in which he participates. The saying of the one condemned to death, "I shall die, I shall live," will then apply to all, even those who never learned to say it themselves in their life. There is no alien sorrow; there is no alien resurrection.

ONCE AGAIN: IVAN AND ALYOSHA

There are two possible answers to extreme suffering in which the afflicted person is struck dumb and learning no longer possible. Dostoevsky has given examples of these answers in *The Brothers Karamazov*. The chapter with the decisive conversation between the two brothers has the heading "Rebellion." Ivan speaks of the suffering of the innocent, of children. "Of the other human tears with which the earth is soaked from its crust to its center, I will say nothing. . . . All that my pitiful, earthly, Euclidean understanding tells me is that there is suffering and that there are none guilty. . . ."[31] He will not accept the explanation that this suffering serves a "higher" or a "future" harmony and is thereby justified. "Besides, too high a price is asked for harmony; it's beyond our means to pay so much for admission. And so I hasten to give back my ticket. . . . It's not God that I don't accept, Alyosha, only I most respectfully return him the ticket." To which Alyosha answers gently, looking down, "That's rebellion."[32]

31. Fyodor Dostoevsky, *The Brothers Karamazov*, the translation by Constance Garnett revised, with an introduction, by Avrahm Yarmolinsky (New York: Heritage Press, 1961), p. 184 (Book Five, Chap. Four).
32. Ibid., p. 186.

Ivan wants to be no rebel. "One can hardly live by rebellion, and I want to live."[33] But as he ponders the suffering of the innocent he is led to rebellion. He, like many of Dostoevsky's characters, is an atheist for love's sake. Alyosha points him to Christ—to the suffering of the one innocent one.

Ivan rebels as he considers suffering, but even Alyosha rejects the idea of purchasing the harmony, the peace, and the rest, at the cost of the death by torture of even one tiny creature. " 'No, I wouldn't consent,' said Alyosha softly."[34]

How is Alyosha's position to be understood? Heinz Robert Schlette has characterized it as "piety," as the position of traditional faith; "the silent, no longer questioning, no longer understanding, but nevertheless humbly obedient submission to the incomprehensible."[35] But is this characterization correct? Nowhere does Alyosha express an absolute agreement, and a future harmony that is paid for with the tears of even one child tortured to death is rejected by him as well as by Ivan. The difference between the two brothers lies in the direction in which each is looking. Ivan rises against the God who causes or allows such suffering. He wants nothing to do with his harmony. His gesture is that of accusation, of rebellion. Alyosha directs his attention not to the power above but to the sufferers. He puts himself beside them. He bears their pain with them. During this conversation he says almost nothing. He listens in agony as Ivan introduces examples of suffering he had assembled as witnesses against the compassion of God. Later Alyosha arises, goes up to Ivan, the rebel and insurrectionist, and kisses him silently on the lips. It is the same gesture with which Christ departs in the legend of the Grand Inquisitor. He is silent, he shares the suffering, he embraces the others. Alyosha's strength is the silent sharing

33. Ibid.
34. Ibid.
35. H. R. Schlette, *Skeptische Religionsphilosophie. Zur Kritik der Pietät* (Freiburg: Verlag Rombach, 1972), p. 145.

of suffering. I don't believe that it is accurate to describe it as "humility" or "submission." God is not over Alyosha, so that he has to submit himself to his incomprehensible lordship. He is within him. Throughout the whole book Alyosha represents the behavior of Christ. If one can speak of humility, then it lies in the fact that his relationship to the sufferers is so strong that all other questions become subordinate. The humility is not over against God. It is the courage to serve others without question or condition. Alyosha couldn't use the picture of the "ticket," which admits one to the theater, because he doesn't see himself as a spectator or a critic. He is one of the actors, and indeed he is always found in the worst spot, where there is suffering and where people are humiliated and put down.

Alyosha does not try to "be conformed to the image of God," which also means demanding a total solution for the world. If the total solution and the complete abolition of suffering is not realizable, then there arises the kind of rebellion Ivan rejects, for, as Dostoevsky sees very clearly, one cannot live in it. Its logical outcome would be suicide, and Ivan's picture of the returned ticket, which, strictly speaking, signifies the rejection of participation in eternal bliss, in the heavenly harmony, is often understood as a total rejection of the conditions under which life takes place here. Understood with this consistency Ivan's gesture is an accusation not only against unjust suffering but, for its sake, against life itself. That Ivan in the unfinished novel contracted brain fever implies this total negation more clearly than an actual suicide could.

The other way is to become Christ's brother. It entails giving up the total solution and shifting attention away from heaven to those who are suffering here. Ivan is metaphysically oriented in his rebellion, Alyosha earthly in his solidarity. One can portray the contrast between the two also in the way in which they hope. Both long for another world, one free of suffering. But what for Ivan is illusion is for Alyosha hope. The difference is minimal. It is no more and no less than our own personal involvement, than participation in the process of actualizing hope. An expectation for the future only becomes hope through entry—via suffering—into the secret that Alyosha designates with the name Christ. The hope that moves a spectator at a game can be an illusion. Only when we ourselves enter the game and bind our own life inextricably to the game's outcome does hope arise. It is not subjectivistic but it does in fact depend on what acting and suffering people do. "In truth each is guilty in all and before all," runs one of the phrases that originate in Russian monasticism. Alyosha tries to live it. Simonov is still living from this tradition. Only love can call itself guilty in this way and take on itself all suffering that we have not prevented or averted. Wherever people suffer Christ stands with them. To put it in less mythological terms, as long as Christ lives and is remembered his friends will be with those who suffer. Where no help is possible he appears not as the superior helper but only as the one who walks with those beyond help. That one bear the burden of the other is the simple and clear call that comes from all suffering. It is possible to help bear the burden, contrary to all talk about a person's final solitude. A society is conceivable in which no person is left totally alone, with no one to think of him and stay with him. Watching and praying are possible.

> Everyone who helps another
> is Gethsemane;
> everyone who comforts another
> is the mouth of Christ.[36]

That people suffer and can be disconsolate is taken for granted here. We should forbid ourselves the dream of a per-

36. From the Russian liturgy, cited from Gottfried Benn, "St. Petersburg, Mitte des Jahrhunderts," *Gesammelte Werke*, Vol. 3 (Wiesbaden: Limes Verlag, 1960), p. 219.

son who needs no consolation. We should also stop classifying suffering merely as something out of the past, for this classification is an act of self-contempt. There is a time for weaping and a time for laughing. To need consolation and to console are human, just as human as Christ was.

We can change the social conditions under which people experience suffering. We can change ourselves and learn in suffering instead of becoming worse. We can gradually beat back and abolish the suffering that still today is produced for the profit of a few. But on all these paths we come up against boundaries that cannot be crossed. Death is not the only such barrier. There are also brutalization and insensibility, mutilation and injury that no longer can be reversed. The only way these boundaries can be crossed is by sharing the pain of the sufferers with them, not leaving them alone and making their cry louder.